"This short but careful, compelling, and ⟨...⟩ great deal, exposing the reason for confli⟨...⟩ amining the biblical terminology in cont⟨...⟩ ......ng the way the theme develops as God's purpose for humanity is progressively disclosed in Scripture. Marny Köstenberger writes with great clarity, showing how a biblical-theological approach to this topic is both necessary and empowering for those who would lead a godly life."

David G. Peterson, Emeritus Faculty, Moore Theological College; author, *Possessed by God*

"This book skillfully summarizes the whole Bible's witness to a highly important doctrine and practical life reality. While readers may differ on particulars, the author builds on the compelling thesis: 'Anyone desiring to grasp God's work in, and call to, sanctification . . . must first come to terms with the glorious, matchless, and undefiled holiness of God.' Study this book for help in understanding how God's holiness pours into and out from the lives of his people through faith in Christ and the Spirit's work."

Robert W. Yarbrough, Professor of New Testament, Covenant Theological Seminary

"The reality that God not only desires but is also at work to accomplish the sanctification of his people cannot be missed in the Bible. But why? And how? And when? In this short but significant book, Marny Köstenberger capably leads readers through Old Testament history, the first coming of the Holy One and his teaching on what holiness of heart looks like, and to the epistles of Paul and Peter and James, which press in the urgency as well as the Spirit's sufficiency to make God's people holy."

Nancy Guthrie, author and teacher, Biblical Theology Workshop for Women

"Marny Köstenberger ably traces the biblical story of the holy God who graciously sanctifies his people for his praise. Sanctification comes at God's initiative, continues by God's power, and culminates in God's glorious presence. Köstenberger explains how positional sanctification empowers believers' progressive growth in holiness through participation in Christ, propelling us toward moral excellence, missional community, and meaningful relationships. I warmly recommend this book!"

Brian J. Tabb, Academic Dean and Professor of Biblical Studies, Bethlehem College and Seminary

"In this informative study, Marny Köstenberger provides an accessible introduction to the important, but often neglected, biblical concept of sanctification. Through a careful analysis of the books of the New Testament, this study offers an engaging exposition of how Jesus Christ bestows on his followers a holy status (positional sanctification) and empowers them to grow in holiness (progressive sanctification). Köstenberger's discussion is especially helpful in addressing the practical implications of holiness for everyday life."

T. Desmond Alexander, Senior Lecturer in Biblical Studies, Union Theological College

"In this comprehensive yet concise treatment of sanctification, Marny Köstenberger masterfully handles the Scriptures to demonstrate that God's call to holiness is clearly presented from Genesis to Revelation. Through careful historical, literary, and theological study, each page unpacks compelling truths that are essential for the individual and corporate Christian life as we await the return of Christ. Köstenberger reminds us that sanctification is not an end in itself; it is given by grace through faith to empower Christ followers to go to the nations. Her thoughtful applications are timeless, making this an essential resource for disciple makers in every cultural context around the world."

Angie Brown, Associate Professor of Women's Ministry, Gulf Theological Seminary, Dubai

"How is it that, throughout history, God takes fallen and broken individuals and makes them into a holy people set apart for himself? Marny Köstenberger takes us on a journey through the Scriptures, exploring both the language and the process of what theologians call the 'doctrine of sanctification.' Characterized by thorough research, this summarization of the author's longtime study and love for the subject examines how and in what contexts God seeks to sanctify or 'holify' us, setting us apart for himself and his purposes in this life and the life to come. I am confident that this volume will be a welcome and worthy addition to the Short Studies in Biblical Theology series."

Theresa Wigington Bowen, Host, Life Impact Ministries; Founder, A Candle in the Window Hospitality Network

Sanctification as Set Apart and Growing in Christ

Short Studies in Biblical Theology

Edited by Dane C. Ortlund and Miles V. Van Pelt

The City of God and the Goal of Creation, T. Desmond Alexander (2018)

Covenant and God's Purpose for the World, Thomas R. Schreiner (2017)

Divine Blessing and the Fullness of Life in the Presence of God, William R. Osborne (2020)

From Chaos to Cosmos: Creation to New Creation, Sidney Greidanus (2018)

The Kingdom of God and the Glory of the Cross, Patrick Schreiner (2018)

The Lord's Supper as the Sign and Meal of the New Covenant, Guy Prentiss Waters (2019)

Marriage and the Mystery of the Gospel, Ray Ortlund (2016)

The New Creation and the Storyline of Scripture, Frank Thielman (2021)

Redemptive Reversals and the Ironic Overturning of Human Wisdom, G. K. Beale (2019)

The Royal Priesthood and the Glory of God, David S. Schrock (2022)

Sanctification as Set Apart and Growing in Christ, Marny Köstenberger (2023)

The Serpent and the Serpent Slayer, Andrew David Naselli (2020)

The Son of God and the New Creation, Graeme Goldsworthy (2015)

Work and Our Labor in the Lord, James M. Hamilton Jr. (2017)

Sanctification as Set Apart and Growing in Christ

Marny Köstenberger

CROSSWAY®

WHEATON, ILLINOIS

Sanctification as Set Apart and Growing in Christ

Copyright © 2023 by Marny Köstenberger

Published by Crossway
          1300 Crescent Street
          Wheaton, Illinois 60187

Cover design: Jordan Singer

First printing 2023

Printed in the United States of America

Trade paperback ISBN: 978-1-4335-7365-1
ePub ISBN: 978-1-4335-7368-2
PDF ISBN: 978-1-4335-7366-8

Library of Congress Cataloging-in-Publication Data

Names: Kostenberger, Marny, 1963– author.
Title: Sanctification as Set Apart and Growing in Christ / Marny Kostenberger.
Description: Wheaton, Illinois : Crossway, 2023. | Series: Short studies in biblical theology | Includes
    bibliographical references and index.
Identifiers: LCCN 2022038670 (print) | LCCN 2022038671 (ebook) | ISBN 9781433573651 (trade
    paperback) | ISBN 9781433573668 (pdf) | ISBN 9781433573682 (epub)
Subjects: LCSH: Sanctification—Christianity.
Classification: LCC BT165 (ebook) | LCC BT165 .K67 2023 (print) | DDC 231.7 23/eng/20230—
    dc20
LC record available at https://www.google.com/url?q=https://lccn.loc.gov/2022038670&source=
    gmail-imap&ust=1674838321000000&usg=AOvVaw2v8CddllJcj52RGWq1Ca2I

Crossway is a publishing ministry of Good News Publishers.

BP		32	31	30	29	28	27	26	25	24	23
15	14	13	12	11	10	9	8	7	6	5	4	3	2	1

For my husband,
Andreas Johannes Köstenberger

Contents

Series Preface

Most of us tend to approach the Bible early on in our Christian lives as a vast, cavernous, and largely impenetrable book. We read the text piecemeal, finding golden nuggets of inspiration here and there, but remain unable to plug any given text meaningfully into the overarching storyline. Yet one of the great advances in evangelical biblical scholarship over the past few generations has been the recovery of biblical theology—that is, a renewed appreciation for the Bible as a theologically unified, historically rooted, progressively unfolding, and ultimately Christ-centered narrative of God's covenantal work in our world to redeem sinful humanity.

This renaissance of biblical theology is a blessing, yet little of it has been made available to the general Christian population. The purpose of Short Studies in Biblical Theology is to connect the resurgence of biblical theology at the academic level with everyday believers. Each volume is written by a capable scholar or churchman who is consciously writing in a way that requires no prerequisite theological training of the reader. Instead, any thoughtful Christian disciple can track with and benefit from these books.

Each volume in this series takes a whole-Bible theme and traces it through Scripture. In this way readers not only learn about a given theme but also are given a model for how to read the Bible as a coherent whole.

We have launched this series because we love the Bible, we love the church, and we long for the renewal of biblical theology in the academy to enliven the hearts and minds of Christ's disciples all around the world. As editors, we have found few discoveries more thrilling in life than that of seeing the whole Bible as a unified story of God's gracious acts of redemption, and indeed of seeing the whole Bible as ultimately about Jesus, as he himself testified (Luke 24:27; John 5:39).

The ultimate goal of Short Studies in Biblical Theology is to magnify the Savior and to build up his church—magnifying the Savior through showing how the whole Bible points to him and his gracious rescue of helpless sinners; and building up the church by strengthening believers in their grasp of these life-giving truths.

Dane C. Ortlund and Miles V. Van Pelt

Introduction

There is a great deal of confusion regarding the nature of sanctification today. In fact, as Steve Porter observes, "an in-depth understanding of spiritual progress has often been lacking within evangelicalism."[1] He refers to church historian Richard Lovelace, who called this "the sanctification gap"—the chasm between people's best intentions and their inadequate understanding of what the Scriptures teach on sanctification. According to Lovelace, evangelicalism, throughout its history, and in keeping with its Reformation heritage, has focused primarily on justification at conversion as well as on general doctrinal orthodoxy and activities such as church involvement, evangelism, and missions. As a result, the tendency within evangelicalism has often been to emphasize the *product* rather than the *process*—doing rather than being, and activity rather than character growth and spiritual development. Porter laments that "in the absence of a robust theology of sanctification, various erroneous models of spiritual growth have emerged that confuse and disillusion many."[2]

---

1. Steve L. Porter, "Sanctification," in *Dictionary of Christian Spirituality*, ed. Glen G. Scorgie (Grand Rapids, MI: Zondervan, 2011), 734. See also Porter's entry "Holiness, Sanctification," in *Dictionary of Paul and His Letters* ed. Gerald F. Hawthorne, Ralph P. Martin, and Daniel G. Reid (Downers Grove, IL: IVP Academic, 1993), 397–402.

2. Porter, "Sanctification," 734–35.

The Language Gap

One reason for this sanctification gap may be the confusion caused by the translation of the Greek terms for "holiness" (*hagiasmos/ hagiosunē/hagiotēs*) and "holy" (*hagios*) with *sanctificatio* and *sanctus* in the Latin Vulgate, which has led to the renderings "sanctification" and "saints" in many, if not most, of our English Bibles. Such renderings, in turn, open up possible connections with Roman Catholic theology and tradition, where "saints" are those who meet special qualifications for holiness. However, while believers doubtless display different levels of maturity, Scripture does not divide people into ordinary Christians and a special category of holy people. Instead, biblically speaking, holiness should set all believers apart from the world and to God. Therefore, to give but one example, it is potentially misleading for English translations to render the Greek term *hagioi* as "saints." Rather, the word is better understood as designating all true believers as "holy ones" regardless of their level of spiritual maturity.

The Tradition Gap

A survey of the literature on sanctification reveals another barrier to understanding, namely, multiple and contradictory perspectives.[3] This plethora of views is the result of varying hermeneutical approaches, views of Scripture, and traditions in different Christian groups or denominations. According to Wayne Grudem, perspectives range from Roman Catholic to Anglican/Episcopalian, Arminian (Wesleyan/Methodist), Baptist, Dispensational, Lutheran, Reformed (Presbyterian), and Renewal (Charismatic/Pentecostal).[4]

---

3. See, e.g., Don Alexander, ed., *Christian Spirituality: Five Views of Sanctification* (Downers Grove, IL: IVP Academic, 1989); Melvin E. Dieter, Anthony A. Hoekema, Stanley M. Horton, J. Robertson McQuilkin, and John F. Walvoord, *Five Views on Sanctification*, Counterpoints: Bible and Theology (Grand Rapids, MI: Zondervan, 1996).

4. Wayne Grudem, *Systematic Theology: An Introduction to Biblical Doctrine*, 2nd ed. (Grand Rapids, MI: Zondervan, 2020), 938–39. See also the resources on the various views in the "Further Reading" section at the end of this volume.

Over the centuries, various traditions formed around differing notions of holiness and sainthood, starting with the New Testament church and continuing through the patristic and medieval periods, and, significantly, the time of the Reformation.[5] Some viewed sanctification primarily as a contemplative and ascetic exercise in the context of monastic spirituality; others conceived it primarily—if not exclusively—in terms of progressive transformation.[6] Some have contended that perfection is achieved upon conversion,[7] while others have argued that a new level of holiness is attained at a second experience of the Holy Spirit subsequent to conversion, a phenomenon sometimes called "second blessing" or "entire sanctification."

The Relevance Gap

A third and final obstacle to understanding sanctification, apart from linguistic confusion and multiple traditions, is apathy. Many people today simply do not care about holiness. The age in which we live is in many ways an irreligious and irreverent age. There is doubtless a "hole in our holiness"—to cite the aptly chosen title of Kevin DeYoung's popular treatment of the topic—at least in part because the whole notion of holiness as being set apart for God and being wholly devoted to serve and worship him has fallen on hard times.[8] For many, talking about holiness seems hopelessly antiquated. There is a demonstrable "relevance gap" in the effort of communicating the concept of holiness to those caught up in the pursuit of pleasure, worldly status, and possessions. Why care? And what is holiness

---

5. Cf. John Calvin, *Institutes of the Christian Religion*, ed. John T. McNeill, trans. Ford Lewis Battles (Philadelphia: Westminster, 1960), 3.3.14 and 3.14.9, who defines sanctification as being "more and more consecrated to the Lord in true purity of life."

6. See, e.g., Porter, "Sanctification," 734.

7. Perfectionism is the belief that, once converted, believers have the ability to live sinlessly. On perfectionism, "second blessing," and "entire sanctification," see Laurence W. Wood, "The Wesleyan View," in *Christian Spirituality*, 95–118.

8. Kevin DeYoung, *The Hole in Our Holiness* (Wheaton, IL: Crossway, 2012).

anyway? For others, a desire for purpose and transcendence leads to "legalism" of a more secular variety: vague spirituality, political tribalism, or even strict diets and exercise regimens fill in for true holiness. It seems we need to start from scratch in educating, and in some cases reeducating, even people in the church as to what holiness is and what the pursuit of it entails.

Starting from Scratch

Starting from scratch is exactly what I aim to do in the present volume. In fact, "start from scratch" is a good way to conceive of biblical theology. What is biblical theology?[9] At its core, it is a way of studying a given topic in Scripture—in our case, sanctification—*on its own terms* and *in its own original context*. Rather than refracting our understanding of what Scripture teaches on sanctification through the Latin Vulgate or a particular faith tradition, I go back to the roots of our Christian faith—the Holy Scriptures—and set out to study the biblical teaching on holiness and sanctification historically, inductively, and, at least initially, descriptively.

That is, I do not start with our own contemporary context or questions—though application is our end goal—but trace how God's people were instructed about holiness *historically*, first in the Old Testament (Israel) and subsequently in the New Testament (the church).

I do not start with an already set theological system or faith tradition and read Scripture through its lenses but attempt to infer and reconstruct the biblical teaching as much as possible by reading and interpreting the relevant texts in Scripture *inductively*.

Finally, I try to connect the dots between the relevant passages as they progressively unfold throughout Scripture and mutually inform

---

9. For a detailed discussion, see Andreas J. Köstenberger and Gregory Goswell, *Biblical Theology: A Canonical, Thematic, and Ethical Approach* (Wheaton, IL: Crossway, 2023), chap. 1.

each other so as to construct a coherent whole—a "biblical theology of sanctification"—*descriptively* before moving on to apply it to our lives today. This is a considerable but not unmanageable task, as I hope to show in this short volume. I believe that such a biblical-theological approach will help avoid much of the confusion that has arisen and unfortunately has kept many from growing in holiness.

The Language of Sanctification

Scripture often uses multiple related words that contribute to its overall portrayal of a concept. For instance, we would be remiss to focus our attention exclusively on the meaning of the single word *sanctify* when there are descriptions of the *concept* of sanctification in Scripture in the form of other words and phrases even where the particular *sanctification* word group is not used.[10] A biblical-theological survey of sanctification, then, commences with a simple word study but does not stop there. An initial immersion into relevant passages will help us absorb the intricacies of the doctrine of sanctification in the context of Scripture.

In this way, we will find bits and pieces of the entire biblical teaching communicated in ways that may be foreign to us in terms of their cultural and historical background and uniqueness. As with a closeup view of a painting's details, we may not immediately perceive the overall picture, but we can nonetheless begin to examine the various colors and textures that make up the beauty of a given doctrine.[11] In the following chapters, as I begin to survey first the Old Testament, and

---

10. Andreas J. Köstenberger with Richard D. Patterson, *Invitation to Biblical Interpretation: Exploring the Hermeneutical Triad of History, Literature, and Theology*, 2nd ed. (Grand Rapids, MI: Kregel, 2020), 516.

11. We will cull the meaning and definition of the relevant words from resources such as Willem A. VanGemeren, ed., *New International Dictionary of Old Testament Theology and Exegesis*, 5 vols. (Grand Rapids, MI: Zondervan, 1997); Johannes P. Louw and Eugene A. Nida, eds., *Greek-English Lexicon of the New Testament: Based on Semantic Domains*, 2 vols. (New York: United Bible Societies, 1989); and Moisés Silva, *The New International Dictionary of New Testament Theology and Exegesis*, 5 vols. (Grand Rapids, MI: Zondervan, 2014), 11.

then the New, I will therefore survey the terminology that together helps us reconstruct the biblical concept of sanctification.

Getting Started

I cannot do much for those who simply do not care about the things of God—irreverence or irreligiousness. But I hope to do my small part in helping to alleviate lack of knowledge or confusion regarding the biblical teaching on sanctification and to stir those who feel in themselves a growing lethargy and desire to be awakened. A greater understanding of what God's word teaches about sanctification will, I trust, lead to a more confident and effective pursuit of holiness, resulting in holier individuals and a holier community of faith. In fact, as we will see, striving for greater holiness is not merely an individualistic quest but has an important relational dimension. What is more, not only is holiness lived out in community; it should also result in mission. With this, I begin where any proper investigation of a matter must necessarily take its point of departure—in the beginning.

1

Foundation

Creation and Covenant

The Bible is the divinely inspired account of God and his relationship with humanity. Genesis and Revelation are the bookends of the great library of Scripture that narrates the story reaching from God's *creation* of the universe and humanity to the new creation. Between these bookends, the Bible provides an account of humanity's fall and God's successive *covenants* with his people, climaxing in the new covenant through Jesus the Messiah.[1] Essentially, the story of God's relationship with humanity is bound up with *presence*: God created humans to live in his presence; they transgressed the Creator's command and consequently were expelled from his presence. In the tabernacle, later in the temple, and ultimately in the Lord Jesus Christ, God manifested his presence. Those who trust in Christ are

---

1. On the series of biblical covenants, see Thomas R. Schreiner, *Covenant and God's Purpose for the World*, Short Studies in Biblical Theology (Wheaton, IL: Crossway, 2017).

reconciled with God, receive the indwelling Holy Spirit, the "other helping presence" (John 14:16), and look forward to eternity spent in God's presence. Being introduced to, and transformed by, the Spirit in the here and now so as to be made fit to live in the presence of God for all eternity is entering the realm of sanctification.

Old Testament Language of Sanctification

Before surveying the Old Testament teaching regarding sanctification, it will be profitable to examine the particular Hebrew words related to holiness. The concept of sanctification is most commonly expressed in the Old Testament through the *qadosh* word group, the Hebrew root word for *holy*, whether noun ("holiness"), adjective ("holy"), or verb ("to make holy, to sanctify").[2] The noun *qōdesh*, "holiness," has the general meaning "be holy, withheld from ordinary use, treated with special care, belonging to the sanctuary." It typically designates "a holy person, thing, place, or time, something sacred, consecrated to God." The term is most commonly found in Exodus 25–Numbers 10; 1–2 Chronicles; and Ezekiel 40–48.[3]

The core meaning is best discerned from key passages in Leviticus and later Ezekiel, which contrast what is holy with what is common or profane. Take Leviticus 10:10, for example: "You are to distinguish between the *holy* and the common, and between the unclean and the clean."[4] When used in conjunction with another noun, the noun functions like an adjective, as in "mountain *of holiness*," that is, "*holy* mountain": "But you who forsake the LORD, who forget my *holy mountain* . . ." (Isa. 65:11; cf. 58:13; 65:25). God is the source of

---

2. Jackie A. Naudé, "*qdš*," in *New International Dictionary of Old Testament Theology and Exegesis*, ed. Willem A. VanGemeren (Grand Rapids, MI: Zondervan, 2012), 3.877–87. See also David Noel Freedman, ed., *The Anchor Bible Dictionary* (New Haven, CT: Yale University Press, 1992), 3:237–49.

3. Naudé, "*qdš*," *New International Dictionary*, 3.877–79.

4. See also Ezek. 22:26; 42:20; 44:23.

all holiness; thus the noun conveys "the essential nature that belongs to the sphere of God's being or activity and that is distinct from the common or profane."[5]

In fact, the term "can be used almost as a synonym of deity" where God is contrasted with his creatures.[6] The expression "holy name," for instance, is virtually synonymous with God: "My *holy name* I will make known in the midst of my people Israel" (Ezek. 39:7; cf. Amos 2:7). Because God is holy, he can deliver his people (Ex. 15:11) and can be trusted to keep his promises (Ps. 105:42). The idea of God's holiness also conveys his moral perfection in contrast to all moral imperfection (Isa. 63:10–11). While holiness is clearly not an integral part of the world, it can operate within it,[7] a reality which has important implications for our understanding of the New Testament call on believers to be in but not of the world.

The adjective *qadosh*, "holy," indicates a dynamic quality rather than merely the "state of belonging to the realm of the divine."[8] It conveys a sense of moving people into the divine realm; while God is the source of all holiness, "human beings can participate in . . . sanctification."[9] In the vast majority of contexts, the adjective is used in conjunction with divine (1 Sam. 6:20; Isa. 43:3; Hab. 1:12) or human beings (Deut. 14:2; 26:19) and the sacrificial court (Ex. 29:31; Lev. 6:16, 26; 7:6; 10:13; 24:9; Ezek. 42:13).[10] On the whole, the adjective conveys the sense that God, in his very essence, is holy and calls his people to be holy as well, identifying the standard by which they can attain holiness.[11] The word is also used in the title "the Holy One of Israel" or simply "the Holy One" (esp. in Isaiah; see, e.g., 43:15; 45:11).

5. Naudé, "*qdš*," *New International Dictionary*, 3.879.
6. Naudé, "*qdš*," *New International Dictionary*, 3.879.
7. Naudé, "*qdš*," *New International Dictionary*, 3.879.
8. Naudé, "*qdš*," *New International Dictionary*, 3.882.
9. Naudé, "*qdš*," *New International Dictionary*, 3.881–82.
10. Naudé, "*qdš*," *New International Dictionary*, 3.881.
11. Naudé, "*qdš*," *New International Dictionary*, 3.882.

The related verb means "to make holy," that is, to (literally) "holify" or "sanctify." This term conveys the state of or transition toward holiness (i.e., consecration). Such consecration involves both entering into communion with the divine realm and being set apart from the worldly domain.[12] While some consider *separation from* the world to be the essential meaning of the verb, more likely separation is the prerequisite for living in accordance with, and being wholly *devoted to*, God's special purposes.[13] Some instances of the verb indicate that touching a holy object makes a person holy himself. Take Exodus 29:37, for example: "Whatever touches the altar shall become *holy*."[14]

Another set of passages refers to the disregard for God's holiness in the context of Israel's disobedience, resulting in dishonor being brought to God's name among the nations. Representative examples are found in Deuteronomy and Ezekiel: "Because you did not treat me as *holy* in the midst of the people of Israel . . ." (Deut. 32:51); "I will vindicate the *holiness* of my great name, which has been profaned among the nations" (Ezek. 36:23; cf. 38:23). Finally, a type of usage relates to people consecrating themselves to perform a sacred task or to be allowed to enter into God's presence, at times after temporary defilement: "*Consecrate yourselves*, therefore, and be *holy*, for I am the LORD your God" (Lev. 20:7).[15]

The word *holy* in the Old Testament is connected with the overall depiction of, and call to, sanctification for God's people. The basic, physical, literal use of the Hebrew word for holiness, *qōdeš*, refers to being "set apart" or "separate."[16] However, the more typical use of *holy*

---

12. Naudé, "*qdš*," *New International Dictionary*, 3.885.

13. Naudé, "*qdš*," *New International Dictionary*, 3.882.

14. See also Ex. 29:21; 30:29; Lev. 6:18, 27.

15. See also Ex. 19:22; Lev. 11:44; Num. 11:18; Josh. 3:5; 1 Sam. 16:5; 2 Sam. 11:4; 1 Chron. 15:12; 2 Chron. 5:11. In these examples, people must prepare themselves before they can meet a holy God and enter into his presence.

16. As Herman Bavinck notes, the root meaning is "to cut, separate" and "expresses the idea of being cut off and isolated." *Reformed Dogmatics: God and Creation*, vol. 2., ed. John Bolt, trans. John Vriend (Grand Rapids, MI: Baker Academic, 2004), 217.

in the Old Testament carries the connotation of religious and moral purity, God's desire for his creatures to be consecrated or devoted to him and thus fit to live in communion with him.[17]

The preceding survey of Hebrew words relating to holiness has set the broad parameters for our study of sanctification in the Old Testament. While biblical theology is more than word studies, this overview has laid a helpful foundation for the remainder of our study. Next, we will turn to the various concepts, time periods, and portions of the Old Testament pertaining to sanctification for a more in-depth investigation.

God's Eternal Holiness

Holiness is first and foremost a divine attribute. God alone is truly holy; there is none like him.[18] The holiness of God is his very "name" (Isa. 57:15) and distinguishes him from his creation (1 Sam. 2:2). God's eternal holiness, and his work on behalf of his people to bring about a derivative holiness in them, is revealed in the Old Testament in a number of ways (cf. Lev. 19:2).[19] The Old Testament depicts God in glowing terms as holy and glorious, whether in his self-descriptions, in pronouncements made about God by various Old Testament characters, or in narrative portions describing the words and works of God.

At the exodus, the song of Moses exults in God by asking, "Who is like you, O LORD, among the gods? Who is like you, majestic in *holiness*, awesome in glorious deeds, doing wonders?" (Ex. 15:11).

---

17. Cf. Peter J. Gentry, "Sizemore Lectures: No One Holy Like the Lord," *Midwestern Journal of Theology* 12, no. 1 (2013): 17–38; Peter J. Gentry and Stephen J. Wellum, *Kingdom through Covenant: A Biblical-Theological Understanding of the Covenants*, 2nd ed. (Wheaton, IL: Crossway, 2018), 362–63.

18. See Matthew Barrett, *None Greater: The Undomesticated Attributes of God* (Grand Rapids, MI: Baker, 2018).

19. The phrase "the Holy One" or "the Holy One of Israel" is found in Isaiah numerous times (see, e.g., Isa. 1:4; 12:6; 41:14; and esp. the throne room vision in Isa. 6:1–6); see also Ex. 3:5–6; 1 Sam. 2:2; and Ps. 99:2–3. Later, Peter calls Jesus "the Holy One of God" (John 6:69).

The psalmist writes, "Ascribe to the LORD the glory due his name; worship the LORD in the splendor of *holiness*" (Ps. 29:2). The book of Isaiah is replete with God's self-descriptions and others' pronouncements regarding God's unmatched holiness. In the throne room vision, the prophet sees angels crying, "*Holy, holy, holy* is the LORD of hosts; the whole earth is full of his glory!" (Isa. 6:1–4). Later, he writes: "'To whom then will you compare me, that I should be like him?' says the *Holy One*" (Isa. 40:25; cf. 44:6–9); "For I am the LORD your God, the *Holy One* of Israel, your Savior" (Isa. 43:3); "I am the LORD, your *Holy One*, the Creator of Israel, your King" (Isa. 43:15); "For thus says the One who is high and lifted up, who inhabits eternity, whose name is *Holy*: 'I dwell in the high and *holy* place'" (Isa. 57:15). The manifestation of the supremacy of God's being and character is revealed in his holiness.[20]

In these and other biblical portrayals of God, we see God characterized as replete with eternal glory and splendor. There is none like him, majestic and awesome, excellent in every way, high and lifted up, filling the earth with his glory. God is to be revered in awe, and all his works praise him. Nothing compares to him. As the Holy One, God is devoted to his people. He is Israel's Redeemer, the first and the last. There is no other God besides him. He inhabits eternity. He is a rock. He is from everlasting. His splendor covers the heavens. As Jonathan Edwards writes:

> Now God is infinitely holy, and infinitely exalted therein, above the holy angels and all creatures; there is not the least tincture of defilement or pollution in the Deity, but he is infinitely far above it; he is all pure light without mixture of darkness; he hates and abhors sin above all things, 'tis what is

---

20. David Peterson, *Possessed by God: A New Testament Theology of Sanctification and Holiness*, New Studies in Biblical Theology (Downers Grove, IL: IVP Academic, 1995), 18.

contrary to his nature. This, his great holiness, has he made known to us by his justice, truth, and faithfulness in all his dispensations towards us, and by the pure holiness of his laws and commands.[21]

Anyone desiring to grasp God's work in, and call to, sanctification, therefore, must first come to terms with the glorious, matchless, and undefiled holiness of God.

Creation in the Image and Likeness of a Holy God

While God is majestic, sovereign, and holy, he enters into relationship with human beings and is devoted to them in love. We've already mentioned that God created humanity in his image and likeness (Gen. 1:26–28). Though there are differing views on the exact meaning of humanity being God's "image," we understand that human beings, simply by being human, represent God and mediate his rule over his creation.[22] The fact that we've been created in God's holy image, however, implies that we're created to reflect his holiness. God's image is related to what we *are*, and "imaging" is something we should *do*. Since there is no one like God, there are, even before the fall, creaturely limits to the holiness and glory that inheres and is being reflected through his image bearers. Nevertheless, as those created in God's image, the man and the woman are to reflect his glory and holiness both individually and in relation to one another.[23]

---

21. Jonathan Edwards, *Sermons and Discourses, 1720–1723*, vol. 10, *The Works of Jonathan Edwards*, ed. Wilson H. Kimnach (New Haven, CT: Yale University Press, 1992), 423–24.

22. For an analysis of Gen. 1:26–28, see Gentry and Wellum, *Kingdom through Covenant*, 215–54.

23. Cf. Paul's portrayal of sanctification of the renewal of the image of God in us, using "image" language in Col. 3:10 ("renewed in knowledge after the image of its creator"); and Eph 4:24 ("the new self, created after the likeness of God in true righteousness and holiness"). On God's original design, see Andreas J. Köstenberger and Margaret E. Köstenberger, *God's Design for Man and Woman: A Biblical-Theological Survey* (Wheaton, IL: Crossway, 2014), 23–41. On creation in God's image, see Richard J. Middleton, *The Liberating Image: The Imago Dei in Genesis 1* (Grand Rapids, MI: Brazos, 2005); Richard Lints, *Identity and Idolatry: The Image of God and Its Inversion*, New Studies in Biblical Theology (Downers Grove, IL: IVP Academic,

God shares his holiness with his creatures in that the holiness that should characterize the people he created is imparted *to* them rather than being produced *by* them in their own strength.[24] Properly understood, therefore, holiness is God's gift to the people he has made. It is the undeserved blessing bestowed on humanity by the Creator out of his abundant grace and goodness.[25] Not only do God's holiness, majesty, and excellence frequently become the grounds of praise in Scripture (e.g., Isa. 43:21), his holiness also calls for imitation on the part of his image bearers so that they reflect his glory (e.g., Lev. 11:44–45; 19:2; cf. Gen. 1:28).

Fall, Flood, Exodus, Covenants with Israel

God's presence initially dwelt amongst the man and woman in the garden amid the perfect creation God had originally fashioned (Gen. 3:8). Having created them in his image for the purpose of ruling the earth for his glory, the Creator expressed a sense of completeness and satisfaction: "God saw everything that he had made, and behold, it was very good" (Gen. 1:31). However, after the fall of humanity into sin and the ensuing breakdown of relationship—including the man's and woman's inability to fulfill their divinely ordained callings—humanity persisted in a state of rebellion against God, resulting in aberrations such as fratricide (Gen. 4:8), polygamy (4:19), and sexual immorality (Gen. 6:1–4). God indicated his abhorrence toward humanity's sin by exacting judgment with the universal flood (Gen. 6–9). A remnant was given reprieve through a covenant established with Noah (Gen. 9:8–17), one in a series of covenants by

---

2015); John F. Kilner, *Dignity and Destiny: Humanity in the Image of God* (Grand Rapids, MI: Eerdmans, 2015); and Peter J. Gentry, "Kingdom through Covenant: Humanity as the Divine Image," *Southern Baptist Journal of Theology* 12, no. 1 (2008): 16–43.

24. Later, Peter would speak of believers becoming "partakers of the divine nature" (2 Pet. 1:4).

25. Michael Allen, *Sanctification*, New Studies in Dogmatics (Grand Rapids, MI: Zondervan, 2017), 88.

which God, by the promise of redemption, held out hope for people who feared him.

While originally having been created for a glorious and fulfilling relationship with God, humanity slid into sin and destruction. Throughout human history, this downfall was manifested in a variety of ways, including sexual immorality, corrupt worship, and irresponsible leadership.[26] And yet humanity's relationship with God awaited future redemption. Initially promised by God immediately following the fall—to be fulfilled in due course in the messianic "seed" (Gen. 3:15), and reiterated and further developed in the Abrahamic covenant (Gen. 12:1–3; 15:1–6, 18; 18:18; 22:15–18)—divine deliverance was enacted at the exodus.[27] God brought his people out of Egyptian slavery into the promised land, gave them the law for obedience, and made the necessary provisions for sacrificial cleansing in case of disobedience (Ex. 12–30).

At the exodus, God "remembered" his covenant made originally with Abraham (Ex. 2:24). As a sign of his love and devotion, God established a covenant with Israel at Mount Sinai in which he made provision for holy living to prepare the people of Israel to meet their God and to enjoy fellowship with him. After forty years of Israel's wandering in the wilderness, God brought the nascent nation across the Jordan and led them to settle in the land promised to their ancestors; there, Joshua renewed the covenant (Josh. 8:30–35). The covenant served not only as a mechanism by which the people of Israel could be cleansed and their sins forgiven but also as a signpost to the righteousness and holiness of God as displayed amongst and through his people before the surrounding nations.

---

26. Andreas J. Köstenberger with David W. Jones, *God, Marriage, and Family: Rebuilding the Biblical Foundation*, 2nd ed. (Wheaton, IL: Crossway, 2010), 31–39.

27. On Gen. 3:15, see Paul Williamson and Rita Cefalu, eds., *The Seed of Promise: The Sufferings and Glory of the Messiah; Essays in Honor of T. Desmond Alexander* (Wilmore, KY: GlossaHouse, 2020).

Despite this promising beginning, however, Israel went on to reject the God of the covenant. God had demonstrated great love and tender concern in the manner in which he had provided redemption—taking his people by the hand and bringing them out of bondage (cf. Jer. 31:32)—yet his gracious covenant was rendered ineffective in accomplishing permanent deliverance. While the laws stipulated in the Mosaic covenant served as expressions of God's holy and righteous character, they remained external standards and regulations that were insufficient to effect heartfelt obedience. Not that the covenant was defective in and of itself; rather, God's people were unable to live by it as their hearts had not (yet) been spiritually transformed. This points to the fallenness of the human condition—including God's chosen people Israel—and the need for further divine provision to enable obedience.

Devotion as Entailment of Holiness

As a people created by God and for God—a people for his own possession—Israel was called to exhibit devotion to the God who had brought the nation out of Egypt and established a covenant with her. Thus holiness served as a key characteristic of the relationship between God and his people. In this way, there is a close connection between Moses's call in Exodus 3 (see esp. v. 5: "the place on which you are standing is holy ground") and Israel's call in Exodus 19 that links God's manifestation of his holiness with his call for his people to pursue holiness as well. On a larger scale, the integral connection between God's own holiness and his call for his people to be holy at the exodus paves the way for the new exodus Jesus would launch through his death on the cross (cf. Mark 1:1–3; Luke 9:31).

Israel existed as a nation belonging to God. This went hand in hand with her consecration in that those who belonged to God were devoted loyally and exclusively to him. Israel was not only a royal priesthood and holy nation but also God's personal treasure and possession (Ex. 19:5–6; applied to the church in 1 Pet. 2:9). This reflected the nature of the nation's intimate relationship with God and her calling from God—they were a mediatorial priesthood and kingdom in God's service and thus were to reflect his holiness.[28]

The notions of consecration and devotion are therefore essential to understanding the term *holy*. As the Israelites' relationship with God was covenantal, it required faith and obedience. God's people were to be committed to him because God had committed himself to them. While God's election and call were undeserved and acts of sheer grace, God's people were nonetheless called to reciprocate by their devotion to God and obedience to him. In this regard, the law not only provided rules for human conduct but regulated people's relationship with God based on the way in which God had created humanity. The Ten Commandments thus do not only express moral principles but serve as "the foundation of true social justice and the basis of what it means to be a son or daughter of God, an Adamic figure—that is, truly and genuinely human."[29]

The Levitical Code and God's Standard of Holiness

In Leviticus the reader is introduced to the concept of holiness through a code that provides a framework for human conduct by consecrating individuals, places, and material objects for God.[30] The Levitical holiness code is regularly punctuated by God's calls for Israel to be holy: "Be holy, for I am holy" (Lev. 11:44–45; 19:2; 20:7, 26). In Leviticus 20:26 God addresses Israel, saying, "You shall be holy to me, for I the LORD am holy, and have separated you from the peoples, that you should be mine." Here we see that Israel belongs

---

28. For a discussion of the phrase "kingdom of priests," see Gentry and Wellum, *Kingdom through Covenant*, 356–62.

29. Gentry and Wellum, *Kingdom through Covenant*, 395.

30. Allen, *Sanctification*, 119.

solely to God and is thus expected to remain wholly and exclusively devoted to him.

God provided the Levitical code for his people Israel in order to instruct them to live in devotion to God and thus be distinct from the surrounding nations. God also provided a mechanism by which sacrifices could be offered for sin and forgiveness be mediated through the high priest. Such individuals were persons devoted exclusively to God's service. Living according to the Levitical holiness code—as mediated by the high priest devoted to God and his service—would make Israel fit for the holy God who dwelt in their midst. Since all of this was done at God's initiative, we can see a most gracious provision for Israel at a time when they were unable to maintain their relationship with the holy Creator God in and of themselves. Both the sacrificial system and the mediation offered by the high priest for the forgiveness of sins served the purpose of preparing people for a devoted relationship with God.

The instructions for holy living given by God in the Levitical code may be misconstrued as legalistic requirements to earn God's favor. However, this was not their purpose. Rather, God meant them for the good of his people, even though Israel proved incapable of keeping them.[31] God's people were unable to maintain holy conduct that allowed them to experience God's presence continually amongst them. However, these instructions were not meant solely or even primarily to accentuate their failure and condemn them such that they could never meet with God again. Rather, God gave them the code as a gift to lead them back to him. Without the help and guidance provided in the Levitical instructions, the

---

31. As Meyer reminds us, even though "the law could not serve as the solution to our sin problem," the "problem was not with the nature of the law but the nature of sinful humanity." Jason C. Meyer, "The Mosaic Law, Theological Systems, and the Glory of Christ," in *Progressive Covenantalism: Charting a Course between Dispensational and Covenant Theologies*, ed. Stephen J. Wellum and Brent E. Parker (Nashville, TN: B&H Academic, 2016), 78.

people of Israel would remain indigent and ignorant about their way back to God.

David Peterson summarizes the Old Testament teaching on sanctification as follows: "In the final analysis, Israel's task as a 'holy nation' was to sanctify the Lord before the nations by responding appropriately to him as the Holy One. God's honor and the salvation of the nations were at stake here. As Israel pursued the path of holiness, God promised to bless her and make her a blessing to the nations."[32] Having been delivered from bondage in Egypt, God's people were given a way to remain in the devoted relationship with God for which they had been created. Their failure to live up to the Levitical holiness code demonstrated that this kind of devoted relationship could not be accomplished by their own efforts. Thus the Old Testament description of their failure serves as a picture for people of all times to see their need for a Redeemer. This Redeemer was the Messiah, to be revealed when the time was right according to God's plan (cf. Gal. 4:4).

God's Continued Work to Restore Israel

God continued to work through the time of the judges to raise up leaders who would return the nation to faithfulness in his covenant. In the refrain lamenting this period in Israel's history—"Everyone did what was right in his own eyes" (Judg. 17:6; 21:25)—we can see that God's people experienced a serious moral and spiritual decline. The judges, who essentially served as national deliverers, did not succeed in bringing the people back to the holy ways of God.

During the united monarchy, God made a covenant with David (2 Sam. 7:12–13) that continued to express his faithfulness to his previous covenants. This covenant specified that the promised

---

32. Peterson, *Possessed by God*, 24.

offspring or "seed"—the Messiah—would be a descendant of David. After David's death, Solomon built the temple as the place where God would manifest his holy presence. Yet, again, Israel failed to live according to the covenants God had established with the nation. After Solomon's death, and because of his sin, the kingdom was divided; both Israel (the northern kingdom) and Judah (the southern kingdom) faced increasing pressure under the Assyrians and Babylonians, respectively. This pressure would lead both parts of the kingdom to break covenant and succumb to idolatry. Thus, both Israel and Judah fell under the curse of the Mosaic covenant, which involved exile (Deut. 28:15–68; cf. 30:1, 19).

Exile from the promised land, in turn, marked God's punishment for the nation's disobedience toward the one who had delivered them from bondage, given them the law, and established a series of covenants to sustain their relationship with a righteous and holy God—Yahweh, who was both their Creator and their Redeemer. How does all of this connect to sanctification? This brief review of Israel's history from creation to exodus and exile reveals as the constant theme Israel's call and covenantal obligation to remain in right relationship with God. And yet, while God had graciously taken the initiative, his people failed to respond to his saving grace in trust and obedience.

The Temple: The Presence, Power, and Holiness of God

Throughout Israel's history, God manifested his presence and glory amid his people in both the tabernacle and the temple. In essence, therefore, the story of humanity in general, and of Israel in particular, is accompanied by the continual manifestation of God's relational presence amongst his people.[33] His glory, holiness, and power identified him as the Creator and Redeemer of Israel who called his people

---

33. See esp. J. Scott Duvall and J. Daniel Hays, *God's Relational Presence: The Cohesive Center of Biblical Theology* (Grand Rapids, MI: Baker, 2019).

to enter into relationship with him. Following the exodus, the Israelites were engaged in constructing the tabernacle, a mobile sanctuary in which God would manifest himself on their journey.

The notion of God's people building a sanctuary for God to indwell first emerged in the aftermath of the exodus: "Let them make me a sanctuary, that I may dwell in their midst" (Ex. 25:8). Soon thereafter, God provided specific instructions for Israel: "Now this is what you shall do to them to consecrate them, that they may serve me as priests" (Ex. 29:1). In that sanctuary, God would meet with the people of Israel, and this place was to be "sanctified" by God's glory; God would "consecrate" both the "tent of meeting" and the altar (Ex. 29:42–46; cf. Lev. 26:11–12).

Later, David's son Solomon was charged with building a more permanent place where God's presence would dwell. The construction of the temple by Solomon is recounted in great length in the book of 1 Kings (chaps. 5–6). At its completion, Solomon summoned Israel's elders and tribal heads to bring the ark of the covenant to Jerusalem (1 Kings 8:5): "And when the priests came out of the Holy Place, a cloud filled the house of the LORD, so that the priests could not stand to minister because of the cloud, for the glory of the LORD filled the house of the LORD" (8:10–11).

Solomon stood by the altar and offered a solemn prayer of dedication (1 Kings 8:22–24). At this, the Lord told him, "I have *consecrated* this house that you have built, by *putting my name there forever*." God charged Solomon to walk closely with him. If he were to succumb to idolatry, God would cut Israel off from the land he had given them (1 Kings 9:1–7). These words proved to be ominously prescient, as Solomon did indeed fail to live a holy life, disobeying God—and Israel followed suit.

The prophet Ezekiel later described God's judgment upon Israel for her disobedience but then also his plan to gather a believing remnant from exile (Ezek. 11:11–12; cf. 8:17). Yet when the prophet interceded, God responded to his people in exile, promising restoration:

> I will gather you from the peoples and assemble you out of the countries where you have been scattered, and I will give you the land of Israel. . . . And I will give them one heart, and a new spirit I will put within them. I will remove the heart of stone from their flesh and give them a heart of flesh, that they may walk in my statutes and keep my rules and obey them. And they shall be my people, and I will be their God. (Ezek. 11:17–20)

This promise began to be fulfilled when Cyrus, the Persian leader, defeated the Babylonians, enabling a remnant to return and rebuild the temple. The rebuilding of the temple is described in the book of Ezra (3:8, 11–12; 5:5; 6:14; cf. Hag. 1–2).[34] Under the leadership of Ezra and Nehemiah, the second temple was completed. God had proven faithful even when Israel had been unfaithful and had restored his people from exile. Yet while the temple was rebuilt, it did not recover all of its former glory, nor did God's glory descend to take up residence in the temple once again.

The Second Temple period spans from the temple's reconstruction to its destruction in AD 70 by the Romans. We can draw a connection between God's glory filling the temple in the Old Testament and the church as God's new-covenant community in the New. Solomon's temple—the place where God's name and glory were to dwell—foreshadowed the Spirit-filling of believers, marking the community of those redeemed by Christ who receive the Spirit at

---

34. On Jesus as the new temple, see Andreas J. Köstenberger, *The Jesus of the Gospels: An Introduction* (Grand Rapids, MI: Kregel, 2020), 379–80.

conversion. The church is the restored people of God and the place where the Spirit corporately dwells.[35]

New Covenant Foretold: The Coming Age of the Spirit

We've seen how God established a series of covenants with Noah, Abraham, and David and in the Mosaic covenant set forth his righteous and holy standards for his people while making provision for disobedience. While God's glory came to dwell amid Israel in the Solomonic temple, however, the nation failed to keep the covenant and thus incurred God's judgment in the form of exile from the promised land. It is at that time that exilic prophets such as Ezekiel and Jeremiah articulated the expectation of a new covenant that would replace the old.

In the last days, God's people would no longer profane his holy name among the nations as they had done prior to the exile. Instead, God would inscribe his law in people's hearts; he would be their God, and they his people. At that time, everyone would intimately know the Lord (Jer. 31:31–34). God would give his people a new heart and a new spirit; he would put his Spirit within them and cause them to walk in his statutes and obey his commandments (Ezek. 36:20–27). Then the nations, likewise, would know that God was the Lord who set Israel apart (Ezek. 37:23–28).

Later, we read in the same prophetic book, "My holy name I will make known in the midst of my people Israel, and I will not let my holy name be profaned anymore. And the nations shall know that I am the Lord, the Holy One in Israel" (Ezek. 39:7). God expressed his great love for his people and his ultimate desire for them to be fully cleansed from all uncleanness. He offered cleansing and the gift of a

35. Andreas J. Köstenberger, "What Does It Mean to Be Filled with the Holy Spirit?," *Journal of the Evangelical Theological Society* 40 (1997): 234.

new heart and declared that he would put his Spirit within them. In this way, he would cause his people to walk in his ways.

While making clear that the human heart is "desperately wicked and deceitful" (Jer. 17:9), Jeremiah also gives hope and provides an explanation as to the manner in which God's people will be enabled to live holy lives in conjunction with the God who created them to be a people for himself. Jeremiah reveals how the new covenant will be superior to the old: God's law will be written on people's hearts— a reference to the indwelling Holy Spirit—and God will remember people's sins no more. The forgiveness procured through the new covenant is both *definitive* and *complete*. Ezekiel and Jeremiah reveal the depth of Israel's—and all humanity's—sin problem as well as the depth of God's coming provision.

Summary

God demonstrated his holiness and desire for his people to reflect his holiness in several ways in Old Testament times. He delivered them from bondage at the exodus. He established a covenant with them in order that they may "belong to him and to fulfill his purpose."[36] He gave them the Levitical code to show them how to maintain purity and righteousness before a holy God. He dwelled in Israel's midst, first in the tabernacle and later in the temple.

However, in view of Israel's failure to keep the terms of the old covenant and to live up to the standard for holiness stipulated in it, exilic and postexilic prophets began to speak of a new covenant in which God would write his law on people's hearts. God would give them a new heart and a new spirit—his own Spirit—who would cleanse, renew, transform, teach, and guide them.[37] In view of this prospect, the role of the Levitical priesthood and sacrificial system

---

36. Peterson, *Possessed by God*, 27.
37. Peterson, *Possessed by God*, 27.

was only preparatory, as was the role of God's temporary dwelling places in the tabernacle and the first and second temples.[38]

Already in the Old Testament, we see a developing picture of the holiness of God and his expectation that his people live holy lives before him. In this chapter, we've explored the way in which the Old Testament shines the spotlight on humanity's need to reflect God's glory and to be wholly devoted to him. We've also seen that the later prophets foresaw a time when God would establish a new covenant with his people. With this, we're ready to move on to the New Testament to learn how the coming of Jesus fulfilled Old Testament messianic expectations and how the Spirit was poured out at Pentecost to usher in the age of the Spirit.

---

38. Cf. Peter W. L. Walker, *Jesus and the Holy City: New Testament Perspectives on Jerusalem* (Grand Rapids, MI: Eerdmans, 1996), 315.

2

Inauguration

God's Kingdom

God's holy dwelling in the midst of his chosen people sets the stage for the New Testament. The holy God visited his chosen people in the incarnation of Jesus, who walked in perfect human holiness. As we enter the New Testament world through the Gospels, we read about the mission of Jesus to Israel as predicted in the Old Testament. The biblical account moves from God's promises to Abraham the Jewish patriarch to Jesus, Abraham's descendant (Gal. 3:16). The book of Acts shows how, based on Jesus's finished work on the cross and God's vindication of Jesus at his resurrection, the gospel spread beyond the Jewish world to the ends of the earth, in fulfillment of God's promises to Abraham (Matt. 28:16–20; cf. Gen. 12:1–3).

New Testament Language of Sanctification

As with our survey of the Old Testament, we begin this section with a survey of the terminology related to sanctification. In the New

Testament, the adjective *hagios* is the primary word translated "holy."
In the plural, *hoi hagioi* literally means "holy people." However, the
word is usually translated as "saints," that is, believers.[1] For example,
Paul begins the letter to the Romans, "To all those in Rome who are
loved by God and called to be *saints*" (Rom. 1:7).[2] *To hagion* and *ta
hagia* mean, literally, "holy thing" or "holy things," respectively. The
expression is typically translated as "holy place" or "holy places," such
as in Hebrews 8:2, where Jesus, in his role as eternal high priest, is
said to be "a minister in the *holy places*" (see also Matt. 7:6; Luke 1:35;
Heb. 9:1–25; 10:19; 13:11).

The word *holy* occurs in conjunction with the following phrases:
"holy Scriptures," "Holy One of God," "holy mountain," "holy city"
(i.e., Jerusalem), "Holy Spirit," "the prayer [or prayers] of the saints
[i.e., holy ones]," and "the holy place" (i.e., the temple). The phrase
hagiai graphai designates the Scriptures as "holy" (Rom. 1:2), while
ho hagios tou theou refers to Jesus as the "Holy One of God" (Mark
1:24; Luke 4:34; John 6:69). *Hagios oros* means "holy mountain"
(2 Pet. 1:18); *hagios polis*, "holy city" (e.g., Matt. 4:5; 27:53). Holiness is also an essential characteristic of the Holy Spirit (e.g., Matt.
1:18–20; Mark 1:8; Luke 1:15; John 1:33; Acts 1:2, 5, 8; 1 Cor. 6:19).
Twice in Revelation we find the phrase "prayer [or prayers] of the
saints" (Rev. 5:8; 8:3–4). Finally, "holy place" occasionally occurs as
a euphemism for the temple (Matt. 24:15; Acts 6:13; 21:28).

Hagiazō is the verbal form of *hagios*, "holy," and means "to make
holy," that is, "to sanctify." First Peter 3:15 may serve as an example:
"In your hearts honor Christ the Lord as *holy*" (literally, "sanctify"
the Lord). Another poignant instance is John 17:17: "*Sanctify* them
in the truth; your word is truth" (cf. Matt. 6:9; Luke 11:2; Rev. 22:11).
The root idea of being devoted to God's holy use is evident in pas-

---

1. On the problematic nature of this rendering, see the introduction.
2. See also Matt. 27:52; Acts 9:13, 32, 41; 26:10; Rom. 8:27; 12:13; 15:25–31; 16:2, 15.

sages such as John 17:19: "For their sake I *consecrate* myself, that they also may be *sanctified* in truth."[3] As we will discuss further below, the sense in which the word is used includes *positional* sanctification (e.g., 1 Cor. 1:2) as well as *progressive* sanctification (e.g., 1 Thess. 5:23).

There are three New Testament nouns for *holiness*, with no discernible difference in meaning. *Hagiasmos* is typically translated as "holiness" or "sanctification." An excellent example of this usage is 1 Thessalonians 4:3–4, 7: "For this is the will of God, your sanctification: that you abstain from sexual immorality; that each one of you know how to control his own body in holiness and honor. . . . For God has not called us for impurity, but in *holiness*."[4] The two other words for "holiness" are *hagiotēs* (2 Cor. 1:12; Heb. 12:10) and *hagiōsunē* (Rom. 1:4; 2 Cor 7:1; 1 Thess. 3:13). These words represent different ways of making an adjective into a noun with the use of different suffixes used possibly for stylistic variation.

In addition to studying the relevant biblical words for "holy" and "holiness," we can engage the *concept* of sanctification more fully as we discover other related words in Scripture. Thus, rather than merely studying the *qadosh* and *hagios* word groups, we can explore relevant semantic domains, that is, word families or groups that broadly relate to sanctification. According to the *Greek-English Lexicon of the New Testament: Based on Semantic Domains*,[5] the New Testament concept of sanctification is expressed by the following range of words: (1) *arētē* ("goodness" in terms of moral excellence); (2) *hagios* ("holy"; see discussion above); (3) *teleios*

---

3. See also Matt. 23:17–19; John 10:36; Acts 20:32; 26:18; Rom. 15:16; 1 Cor. 1:2; 6:11; 7:14; Eph. 5:26; 1 Thess. 5:23; 1 Tim. 4:5; 2 Tim. 2:21; Heb. 2:9–11; 9:13; 10:10, 14, 29; 13:12.

4. See also Rom. 6:19, 22; 1 Cor. 1:30; 2 Thess. 2:13; 1 Tim. 2:15; Heb. 12:14; 1 Pet. 1:2.

5. Johannes P. Louw and Eugene A. Nida, eds., *Greek-English Lexicon of the New Testament: Based on Semantic Domains*, 2 vols. (New York: United Bible Societies, 1989). I have slightly adapted the entries from this resource below so the entries appear without quotation marks, especially with regard to punctuation.

("perfect"/"perfection" or mature behavior); and (4) *pneumatikos* ("spiritual").[6]

Studying these related words helps us expand our study of the concept of sanctification from the original *word* study of the word *hagios*, "holy," to a study of the *concept* of holiness, which is expressed by these other related words: "goodness" (moral excellence), "perfect," "mature," or "spiritual." In addition, there may be other potentially related words that reflect an aspect of sanctification, such as "grow" (*auxanō*), "walk" (*peripateō*), or "bear fruit" (*karpophoreō*).

The word *arētē* denotes moral excellence, goodness, or virtue.[7] The expression is found in Philippians 4:8: "If there is any *moral excellence*, if there is [reason for] praise . . ." (author's translation); and 2 Peter 1:3, which refers to God as the one who has "called us to his own glory and excellence" (see also 1:5).

The *hagios* word group has already been discussed above.[8] The word means "holy ones" and is often translated as "saints." However, *hagioi* is used for all those saved, born again, and set apart for God regardless of their level of maturity. This observation is rather startling. We know that in reality no believer is ever perfectly holy in the flesh, yet we as believers are still called that—holy ones! The very identity of believers, the essence of those who are born again, is encapsulated in what they are called: "holy." This constitutes a challenge to all of us, a wake-up call to live in keeping with what we're already called, to be what we are in Christ—holy.

The word *teleios* can mean either "perfect" or "mature."[9] Where it denotes perfection, it refers to a person who does not lack any virtuous quality. James 3:2 may serve as an example: "If anyone does not stumble in what he says, he is a perfect man" (cf. Matt. 5:48:

---

6. Louw and Nida, *Greek-English Lexicon*, 742.
7. Louw and Nida, *Greek-English Lexicon*, 744.
8. Louw and Nida, *Greek-English Lexicon*, 745.
9. Louw and Nida, *Greek-English Lexicon*, 746.

"You therefore must be perfect, as your heavenly Father is perfect").
The related noun *teleiotēs* is found in Colossians 3:14 and translated
in various ways: "In addition to all these, love, which is the bond of
perfection" or "which produces perfect unity" or "which binds all
things together in perfect unity." A slightly different but related nu-
ance is that of maturity in thought or conduct. Consider Hebrews
6:1: "Therefore let us leave the elementary doctrine of Christ and go
on to maturity" (cf. Heb. 10:1; 1 John 2:5); and Ephesians 4:13, which
speaks of believers growing "to mature manhood, to the measure of
the stature of the fullness of Christ." The idea of perfection indicates
the goal toward which believers are to strive in sanctification, the
idea of attaining full maturity. Peterson states that "the terminology
of perfection is used to proclaim the fulfillment or consummation
of men and women in a permanent, direct and personal relationship
with God. . . . Our sanctification or consecration to God is only a
part of the process of eschatological perfection, achieved through
the perfecting of Christ ([Heb.] 2:10; 5:9; 7:28)."[10]

Another important dimension of sanctification/holiness is
conveyed by the *pneumatikos* ("spiritual") word group.[11] The term
spiritual is used in Scripture to describe the work of the Spirit in humanity, as the energizing source for the resulting maturity or growth
in believers' lives.[12] In view of the fact that the Spirit is the primary
agent of sanctification, it is crucial to learn about the Spirit's role and
work in the life of the believer. Thus 1 Corinthians 2:13 speaks of
explaining spiritual truths to those who possess the Spirit. The expression "spiritual" or "from the Spirit" may in various contexts refer
to spiritual gifts, blessings, or other matters pertaining to the work

---

10. David Peterson, *Possessed by God: A New Testament Theology of Sanctification and Holiness*, New Studies in Biblical Theology (Downers Grove, IL: IVP Academic, 1995), 36–37.

11. Louw and Nida, *Greek-English Lexicon*, 143.

12. See Gregg R. Allison and Andreas J. Köstenberger, *The Holy Spirit*, Theology for the
People of God (Nashville, TN: B&H Academic, 2020), who provide a thorough biblical and
theological discussion of the work of the Spirit in sanctification.

of the Holy Spirit. Consider 1 Corinthians 12:1: "Now concerning spiritual gifts, brothers, I do not want you to be uninformed" (i.e., about gifts that come from the Spirit).

One quarter of the instances of *hagios* in the New Testament are found in Acts, and the term also occurs with particular frequency in Ephesians. What is more, whereas the Old Testament frequently refers to God as holy, the New Testament does so only infrequently (e.g., John 17:11; 1 Pet. 1:16; Rev. 4:8; 6:10). Jesus Christ is referred to as holy in the same way as God only once: "The words of the holy one, the true one . . ." (Rev. 3:7), though there are many other associations to holiness found elsewhere in Scripture.[13] While some passages in the New Testament retain the Old Testament frame-work, however, "the concept of holiness in the NT is determined rather by the Holy Spirit, the gift of the new age[,] . . . and sacred no longer belongs to things, places, or rites, but to manifestations of life produced by the Spirit."[14] Believers must learn about and depend upon the Spirit.[15]

It is helpful to look at these clusters of words that have a bearing on our understanding of the Bible's teaching on sanctification. In this regard, as we've seen, "spiritual" essentially refers to someone who has received God's Spirit and lives accordingly and is used also to describe that which is derived from the Holy Spirit in general. As we'll explore later in this volume, the term *spiritual* relates to the New Testament teaching on believers' union with Christ. It also relates to the New Testament emphasis on the presence and work of the Holy Spirit in believers' lives.[16] The New Testament teaching on spiritual gifts is also highly significant for our experience of spirituality. Spiri-

---

13. Moisés Silva, *New International Dictionary of New Testament Theology and Exegesis*, 5 vols. (Grand Rapids, MI: Zondervan, 2014), 1:128.

14. Silva, *New International Dictionary*, 1:129.

15. Silva, *New International Dictionary*, 1:130.

16. Andreas J. Köstenberger, *Excellence: The Character of God and the Pursuit of Scholarly Virtue* (Wheaton, IL: Crossway, 2011), 69; see also chap. 4 for a discussion of spirituality.

tual gifts, endowed upon the believer for the sake of building up the local church, represent a unique and vital expression of spirituality in a believer's life. Withholding one's gifts would be tantamount to being unspiritual, though the use of spiritual gifts does not comprise the totality of life in the Spirit.

God's Kingdom and the "Greater Righteousness"

Having surveyed the language of sanctification in the New Testament, we're ready to turn to the new-covenant writings for a closer look. The Gospels are the glue between Old Testament promises and New Testament fulfillment: "All four Gospels take their conscious point of departure from the Hebrew Scriptures and from God's acts in history and his promises to his chosen servants."[17] Jesus himself does not teach explicitly about sanctification except by implication, as in the Sermon on the Mount (Matt. 5–7). There, he interprets the law and explains its higher purpose by giving specific examples in the context of his teaching on the coming kingdom of God. In the Johannine farewell discourse, Jesus anticipates his return to the Father and instructs his followers about their need to sustain an organic union with him through the Spirit (John 15:1–10). His final prayer prior to his departure identifies the consecration and commissioning of his followers as a major purpose for his coming (John 17:17–18).

Jesus's words in the Sermon on the Mount provide essential instruction for his followers—a new holy people for the coming kingdom. While Jesus's emphasis on the kingdom of God is expressed in all five major discourses featured in Matthew, the Sermon on the Mount is Jesus's inaugural address and sets forth in programmatic

---

17. Andreas J. Köstenberger with Richard D. Patterson, *Invitation to Biblical Interpretation: Exploring the Hermeneutical Triad of History, Literature, and Theology*, 2nd ed. (Grand Rapids, MI: Kregel, 2020), 165–66.

fashion the characteristics of God's kingdom. Jesus's instruction on the mountain recalls the giving of the law on Mount Sinai; as the Israelites were to be a distinct and holy people, Jesus's followers were to be salt and light, a city on a hill, a distinct and holy people. The Beatitudes display this distinction and reflect kingdom attitudes—humility, mourning for sin, meekness, hunger and thirst for righteousness, mercy, purity of heart, peacemaking, and bearing up under persecution (Matt. 5:3–11). Jesus himself lives out these realities and serves as an example for his committed followers. Nevertheless, a high regard for the law is apparent even at this new stage of salvation history. Jesus insists that he didn't come to abolish the law but to fulfill it (Matt. 5:17). Similarly, New Testament believers should not ignore the basis of their faith in Judaism. While recognizing the law's limitations, believers should appreciate its contribution to their experience of God and its vital role in their quest to get to know him better.

Yet while Matthew presents Jesus's demand for righteousness in continuity with the law, he reveals new insight about a standard that goes *beyond* the law—a greater righteousness (Matt. 5:20). Correspondingly, Matthew depicts Jesus as the "greater Moses" whose ethical teaching exceeds that given in the law. What's more, while God used Moses to deliver his people from physical bondage in Egypt at the exodus, Jesus came to deliver God's people spiritually and definitively through a new exodus, accomplished through his death on the cross. The Sermon on the Mount also depicts Jesus as a "greater David," instructing his kingdom people in the law as Israel's kings were called to do.[18] His repeated refrain, "You have heard it said," followed by quotes of specific portions of the law—or at least the way in which contemporary Jews interpreted it—is regularly accompanied

---

18. On this point, see Patrick Schreiner, *Matthew, Disciple and Scribe: The First Gospel and Its Portrait of Jesus* (Grand Rapids, MI: Baker Academic, 2019), esp. 103–8.

by, "But I say to you," enunciating a deeper truth underlying a given command (Matt. 5:21, 27, 31, 33, 38, 43).

What is continually in view in these statements is the condition of people's *hearts*. The heart response described is, in fact, meant to be the core of the requirements given in the law (Deut. 6:5; Matt. 22:36–38). Apart from this heartfelt obedience, the acts of obedience previously required by the law are ineffectual. In fact, this inner heart involvement is far more important than mere adherence to the external requirements of the law. This is the "greater righteousness" to which Jesus's followers are to aspire, greater even than that touted by the Jewish religious authorities of his day. Jesus proceeds to open for his followers a new and fresh vision for righteousness that is vitally connected to the inner person. With regard to the specific attitudes to be manifested as expressions of the greater righteousness demanded by Jesus, this vision includes controlling one's anger, pursuing sexual purity, honoring the covenant of marriage, speaking with honesty and integrity, refraining from taking revenge, loving and praying for one's enemies, and avoiding hypocrisy in the practice of one's giving, prayer, and fasting.

The point is for Jesus's followers to live in ways that bear the fruit of righteousness in their actions and words, not merely to engage in meaningless superficial observance of the law. Believers are thus those reclaimed by God as his special possession and called into his service. They are the ones who are called already to live as citizens of the kingdom in anticipation of what awaits them in heaven:

> Grasping Jesus's teaching on God's kingdom isn't so much an intellectual challenge as something requiring spiritual insight. Essentially, Jesus came down from heaven to show us, in his three and a half years of public ministry, what heaven is like. As Revelation tells us, heaven will be a place where "there

will be no more death" or mourning or crying or pain. So when Jesus heals the sick and even raises the dead, he shows us what living forever in God's presence will be like. No one will die; no one will get sick. There'll be no more suffering or sorrow. In short, Jesus gives us a sneak preview of heaven.[19]

In the meantime, Jesus's followers are called to help advance God's kingdom. As Jesus said, "Seek first the kingdom of God and *his* righteousness, and all these things will be added to you" (Matt. 6:33). Righteous living relates to a heart oriented toward God, living in a manner that is completely devoted to righteousness and glory *for him*. However:

> Many of us are still busy building our own "kingdom" while asking Jesus to bless our efforts! We use pious, spiritual language, rationalizing it's all about *him*—when, more often than not, our "kingdom" work may be mostly about *us*. It shouldn't be so. Following Jesus entails submitting to *his* authority. We need to let *him* call the shots and be content to be soldiers in his spiritual army. In this way, already now we're preparing for living in God's kingdom—the supreme, unchallenged reign of God for all eternity.[20]

As we continue our study, we'll add facets to the foundational instructions for spiritual and practical life enunciated in the Sermon on the Mount. For now, we've seen how deeply the inner person is to be connected to righteous living and how this higher standard of obedience to God involves the heart. This heartfelt obedience—far exceeding mere external compliance—is central to kingdom living.

---

19. Andreas J. Köstenberger, *The Jesus of the Gospels: An Introduction* (Grand Rapids, MI: Kregel, 2020), 89.

20. Köstenberger, *Jesus of the Gospels*, 90.

Jesus and the Temple

As the Sermon on the Mount is Jesus's instruction for a new holy people, his body is depicted in John as the new holy sanctuary, the new temple (John 2:18–21; 4:19–24).[21] Jesus's first visit to Jerusalem recorded in John's Gospel finds him clearing the temple. When Jesus, in righteous anger, declares that God's house should be a house of prayer rather than a den of robbers, he indicates the inadequacy of the temple as a place where God and his glory are to dwell. While, as mentioned in the previous chapter, the temple had been rebuilt after the return of a remnant of exiled Jews, the glory of the Lord no longer remained there. The corrupt priesthood and the use of the temple for commercial pursuits tainted it with unrighteousness so that the holy God refused to dwell in this sanctuary.

Nevertheless, the Jewish authorities challenged Jesus's authority over the temple, demanding a sign. Jesus replied, "Destroy this temple, and in three days I will raise it up" (John 2:18). Yet while the authorities surmise Jesus is speaking about the earthly temple, John tells us, "he was speaking about the temple of *his body*" (John 2:21). Here we see the Old Testament temple theme carried a decisive step further. The temple's destruction—which from John's vantage point has already occurred—is tragic enough; but Jesus makes clear that this was only a portent of the "destruction" of Jesus's body in crucifixion, followed by his resurrection on the third day. John is, in effect, saying, "Forget the temple. Believe in the crucified and risen Jesus and worship him!"

The story of Jesus's encounter with the Samaritan woman only a couple chapters later expands on this theme (John 4:19–24). While the Jews worshiped in Jerusalem, the Samaritans had set up a rival sanctuary on Mount Gerizim. Yet their attempt to restore worship

---

21. For the Old Testament context, see the discussion of the temple at the end of the previous chapter.

was unsuccessful. As Jesus tells the Samaritan, true spiritual worship is to be offered neither in Jerusalem nor in any other physical location. Rather, worship is a matter of spirit and truth because God is spiritual in nature. Thus, proper worship ought to be offered in a spiritual manner rather than being tied to a particular building or location; it must occur in the spiritual realm. There is no need to get tied to externals; as Jesus had explained in the Sermon on the Mount, a right relationship with God is a matter of the heart.

The implications of Jesus being the new temple are revolutionary for the New Testament teaching on sanctification. We see that God's presence is uniquely and exclusively manifested in and through Jesus, the only Son of God, the Word made flesh who took up residence amid God's people and uniquely revealed the Father (John 1:14, 18). This Jesus is also the only way to God; there is no access to the Father apart from him (John 14:6). In fact, Jesus and the Father are one (John 10:30). From Jesus's deity and unity with the Father flow our need to believe in Jesus and to be united to him. This becomes clear in Jesus's Farewell Discourse, as we'll see below.

Consecration and Cleansing of the New-Covenant Community

As the Lord called his old-covenant people to be holy, so Jesus called his followers to be holy. Jesus consecrated himself for his mission and consecrated his followers for their mission as well. David Peterson draws attention to several passages in John's Gospel that highlight this consecration for mission in the world:

> In the Gospel of John, Jesus uses the language of sanctification with reference to his own role as the savior and sanctifier of others (Jn. 10:36; 17:19). A comprehensive picture of the sanctification he makes available is then set out in the prayer

of John 17. Delivered in the presence of his Jewish disciples, this prayer promises a sanctification fulfilling and surpassing the sanctification experienced by Israel under the Law.[22]

In the first half of the Gospel, Jesus lodges the claim that God himself set him apart and sent him into the world. When he is about to be stoned on account of blasphemy for allegedly "making himself out to be God," he tells his opponents, "Do you say of him whom the Father consecrated and sent into the world, 'You are blaspheming,' because I said, 'I am the Son of God'?" (John 10:36). This is a momentous declaration of Jesus's otherworldly origin, divine consecration, and commissioning in eternity past. Then, toward the end of his mission on earth, the risen Jesus tells his followers, "As the Father has sent me, even so I am sending you" (John 20:21).

Highlighting these passages helps us identify theological bookends that reveal God's consistent practice of consecrating his own and commissioning them for service. Just as Jesus was sent by God to bring redemption to the world, so he sends his followers into the world to continue his mission. In his obedient and faithful representation of his sender, Jesus serves as a paradigm for the mission his followers are called to accomplish. They, too, are to live their lives as obedient and faithful representatives of their sender, the Lord Jesus Christ, as they share the good news of salvation with a world that languishes in spiritual darkness.

In the middle of John's Gospel, in the footwashing scene, Jesus predicts his imminent departure and explains what this means for his followers' sanctification. He stresses the disciples' need for ongoing cleansing despite the fact that they are already clean by virtue of their decision to follow Christ. At the footwashing, Peter serves as the foil for Jesus's spiritual instruction, whereby the verb "to wash" carries

---

22. Peterson, *Possessed by God*, 28.

a double meaning, referring both to washing his disciples' feet and cleansing his disciples from sin (John 13:3–11). In this object lesson comparing physical and spiritual cleansing, Jesus indicates that Peter has no need to have his whole body washed—his hands and head—but only his feet, because he has already had a full bath. This imagery depicts Peter's complete and final (positional) cleansing by the saving work of Christ; as Jesus noted, Peter is "completely clean." The "cleansing of feet," however, will need to continue on a regular basis, referring to the need for consistent and ongoing spiritual cleansing (i.e., progressive sanctification).

Abiding in Christ

In the bulk of the Farewell Discourse, following the footwashing and culminating in his final prayer, Jesus has sanctification on his mind. Even though he has yet to be crucified, to be buried, to rise from the dead, and to ascend to the Father, he anticipates his glorification and exaltation (his "lifting up") and talks to his followers about life in the Spirit, who will come subsequent to his departure. Jesus himself will "go to prepare a place" for his disciples (John 14:2); yet he will not leave them as orphans—"I will come to you" (14:18). Jesus was *with* his disciples during his earthly ministry, but upon his departure the Spirit would take up residence *in* them.

At this juncture, his disciples are perplexed and confused. Yet, undaunted, Jesus assures them that it will be *better* for them if he goes away, because he will send "another Helper," the Holy Spirit, who will be with them forever (John 14:16). This indwelling Spirit will teach them all things and bring to their remembrance all Jesus has taught them (14:26). He will bear witness to Jesus with and through the disciples (15:26–27) and "convict the world concerning sin and righteousness and judgment" (16:8). In addition, the Spirit will guide them in all the truth and declare to them the things that are yet to come (16:13).

In the allegory of the vine and the branches (John 15:1–11), Jesus tries to help his followers understand how the Spirit's work in them will enable them to stay closely connected both to him and to the Father through him. Jesus's teaching on the coming of the Holy Spirit and believers' organic spiritual union with Christ is foundational for the New Testament teaching on sanctification. What was hard for Jesus's original followers to imagine prior to the Spirit's descent—but what we as Spirit-filled believers have come to experience—is that believers can be united with Christ in the Spirit and thus live in close communion with God even though Jesus is no longer physically present with them.

On the eve of Jesus's departure, he encourages his disciples that he will remain in them even though he is about to depart. He then encourages them to remain in him:

> John's "abiding" theology fleshes out how believers will be able to *sustain* spiritual communion with Christ subsequent to his ascension. In its original setting—the farewell discourse, which is unique to John's Gospel—Jesus is shown to prepare his followers for the period following his exaltation subsequent to the events surrounding the crucifixion (e.g., Jn 14:12, 28).[23]

The language of *dwelling* or *abiding* pervades chapter 14 of John's Gospel. At the very outset, Jesus tells his followers, "In my Father's house are many rooms [literally, 'dwellings,' *monai*, plural noun form of 'abide']. If it were not so, would I have told you that I go to prepare a place for you?" (14:2). When Philip asks Jesus to show him the Father, Jesus replies, "Do you not believe that I am in the Father and the Father is in me? The words that I say to you I do not speak on my own

---

23. Andreas Köstenberger, "Abide," in *Dictionary of Jesus and the Gospels*, 2nd ed., ed. Joel B. Green, Jeannine K. Brown, and Nicholas Perrin (Downers Grove, IL: IVP Academic, 2013), 2.

authority, but the Father who dwells [*menō*, verb form of 'abide'] in me does his works" (14:10). Then, after assuring his disciples that he will not leave them as orphans (14:16), he tells them, "If anyone loves me, he will keep my word, and my Father will love him, and we will come to him and make our home [*monē*, singular noun form of 'abide'] with him" (14:23). While Jesus leaves to prepare an abode for his disciples, he will abide in them by the Spirit, even as he abides in the Father.

John 15, likewise, is replete with *abiding* terminology, containing as many as ten references. Jesus's and the disciples' love and joy are stressed in this section, where "abide" is the operational term for mutual interrelating. Believers abide in Christ and his love, and he in them. This *abiding* language, in turn, is firmly grounded in Old Testament terminology. The historical background to the word that forms the essence of its meaning is the "OT teaching that 'God remains forever' (Ps 9:7), as do his authority, counsel and word (Ps 33:11; 102:12; Is 40:8)."[24] Believers are united with Christ through steadfast abiding in him and his teaching. In this way, they are forever connected to him.

Not only are believers to remain in Jesus, but he will remain in them. The picture of the vine and the branches depicts Jesus as the originating source and the disciples as the dependent branches extending out from the stalk of the vine. Abiding *in him* means that Jesus is the conduit of nurture for any resulting fruit. Just as a branch withers apart from the vine, so will those who are separated from him. Such withered branches are useless and destined to be burned. Those who are genuine Christians should expect to bear fruit, as well as a certain amount of pruning.

Even disciples can produce nothing of spiritual value apart from a purposeful and continued connectedness to Christ. Not only must

---

24. Köstenberger, "Abide," 1.

Christ abide in them, but his word must abide in them as well. As they dwell on his teaching, they are transformed and grow spiritually in keeping with Christ's purposes. In this way, the Spirit and the word work in tandem. An abiding union with Christ avails believers of divine resources so that they may ask whatever they wish, and it will be done for them. As they remain closely connected to Christ, their requests will be honoring and acceptable to God and thus worthy of being fulfilled.

Disciples prove themselves to be such by bearing fruit (John 15:6), and it is by bearing *much* fruit that they glorify the Father. The abundance of fruit may be related to them asking as Jesus encourages them to request anything they desire. Conversely, disciples who produce *little* fruit may display a problem with abiding and thus the need for pruning, which the Father, the vinedresser, will perform in order to enable them to produce more fruit. Those who do not bear *any* fruit are likely not genuine disciples and may not have been born again spiritually. They are branches that are taken and thrown away so that they wither and are cast into the fire to be burned (15:2, 6).

Jesus concludes his comments on abiding by affirming his love for his followers and assuring them of his commitment to their ongoing union with him (John 15:10). He acknowledges that the kind of love he is expressing toward his disciples is like the Father's love for him and reflects the same concrete commitment. This points to the magnitude of devotion he has toward the disciples. The disciples' love for Christ should be exhibited in their continual obedience to his commands, reflecting Jesus's abiding in the Father and his obedience to the Father's commands. Obedience is not foisted on the disciples; their motivation for obedience should be Jesus's great love and desire for them to have fullness of joy. Abiding in Christ's love seems to envisage one basking in the greatest love ever shown, where mutual commitment is assumed yet not demanded. However, it is in reality a privilege—a gift—to abide in Christ and to live a life of obedience to Christ. This abiding obedience is the key to experiencing the fullness of joy for which we were created.

How does one practically abide in Christ? First, abiding in Christ means remaining in his *word* and doing what it says—obedience. This is important to remember in that spirituality is sometimes defined in terms of a mystical union with God in Christ that is insufficiently related to Jesus's teachings and Christian Scripture. This truth is powerfully driven home by Jesus himself at a time when "many believed in him" (John 8:30). Knowing that not all belief is genuine faith, Jesus told the Jews who had "believed" in him, "*If you abide in my word*, you are truly my disciples, and you will know the truth, and the truth will set you free" (8:31–32). Thus believing in Jesus inexorably entails abiding in his word. This is the true meaning of discipleship: tethering one's life to Jesus's teachings and obeying them. In addition, abiding in Christ also means remaining in his *love*, which, as John tells us, also entails loving one another. An *unholy* Christian is a contradiction in terms, as is an *unloving* Christian. Jesus's followers are commanded to love one another the way Jesus loved them—the "new commandment" (13:34–35).

Final Prayer and Commissioning

After this, Jesus prays to the Father for his disciples, reflecting on the earthly mission with which God entrusted him (John 17).[25] Here, Jesus intercedes for his followers, aiming to prepare and equip them for his death and subsequent departure and for life in the Spirit. He prays for the continuing mission he is about to entrust to his disciples. In so doing, he commits to the Father the work he has completed in his ministry amongst them. Having been given this

---

25. For a discussion of Jesus's final prayer, see Andreas J. Köstenberger, "The Context of Jesus' Prayer," *Tabletalk* (December 2020): 4–11.

ministry by the Father, Jesus recognizes the Father's sovereignty in all he has accomplished.

In many ways, Jesus here sets an example for believers regarding the mission they should undertake. He identifies the disciples as those given to him by God for the purpose of coming to know the only true God and Jesus Christ whom he has sent. He prays for them and those who will come to faith through their ministry. As those consecrated and commissioned by Jesus, they are to make God known to others as his duly authorized, faithful, and obedient representatives.

Sanctification language is particularly pronounced at the end of Jesus's prayer for his followers: "They are not of the world, just as I am not of the world. *Sanctify* them in the truth; your word is truth. As you sent me into the world, so I have sent them into the world. And for their sake I *consecrate* myself, that they also may be *sanctified* in truth" (John 17:16–19). Jesus's followers are "not of the world," because they have been spiritually set apart for his service. In fact, Jesus was consecrated by the Father, and consecrated himself, so that his followers might likewise be consecrated and set apart (cf. 10:36). Note that sanctification here entails not merely *personal* holiness— though this is an indispensable prerequisite—but also a *missional* purpose. Jesus's followers are not merely set apart to be holy; they are set apart so they can bear witness to the salvation wrought in Jesus to a lost and dying world. The realm in which this sanctification takes place is "the truth," which is God's word: "Your word is truth" (17:17).

The prayer Jesus offers for his disciples is tantamount to a dedication, a kind of setting apart for service, so that the disciples will be sustained and make an impact on the world by being one with the Father and Jesus, and by imitating Jesus in his mission as those who were sent into the world by him. Jesus indicates that it is the word of God that will enable them to abide—to continue in his ways and be consecrated for service—with a resulting unity that will make a deep impact on the watching world. Though they are not part of this world, Jesus still prays that they will be sanctified in his word. This indicates believers' need for spiritual truth and nurture in order to remain strong in their faith and witness.

Jesus prays for his followers—as well as for those who will believe in him at a later time because of their witness—portraying them as those who, like him, are not of this world (John 17:16). Though not *of* the world, he himself sends them *into* the world, just as God sent him into the world (17:18), praying that they will be kept from the evil one. The prayer for unity shows the importance of community, underscoring the fact that they were to be in the world but not of it, not merely individually but *as a group of people*—to be a unified, set-apart, God-sustained community in the world. In unity, they were to experience something analogous to that which the triune Godhead also experiences and to do so as those who are personally and relationally grounded in the Godhead. This unity is key to their spiritual effectiveness in mission.

The world hates them just as it hates God—the result of being different and set apart—yet Jesus prays that believers will be spiritually preserved amid the ever-present spiritual battle, the powerful downward pull toward spiritual destruction and cultural assimilation. In that context, Jesus prays that God will sanctify his followers in the truth—God's word—and that he will keep them from the evil one. Jesus's desire is that they remain spiritually distinct and separate from the world and remain in him. After his resurrection, Jesus formally sends his disciples, just as he prayed: "As the Father has sent me, so I am sending you" (John 20:21). The disciples' unity with Jesus in the Spirit sanctifies them to undertake a mission like his own. Life in the Spirit is life on mission—following Jesus for the glory of God.

Summary

Our study of the Gospels regarding sanctification has focused on Jesus's Sermon on the Mount and his teaching in the Johannine Farewell Discourse. In the Sermon on the Mount, Jesus articulated the characteristics of the citizens of God's kingdom—the Beatitudes—and upheld a greater righteousness for his followers, a new holy people.

While Jesus does not explicitly mention the Spirit as the agent of sanctification in believers' lives, he makes clear throughout the Sermon on the Mount that God's primary concern is with people's hearts rather than external expressions of piety. This flows from the realization that human hearts are corrupt ever since the fall so that only a deep-seated heart change and heartfelt obedience will satisfy God's demand for holiness and purity in our lives.

In his final prayer, Jesus models the pattern of consecration—being set apart for mission by God—followed by a time of equipping and subsequent commissioning and sending out into the world. This was the way in which Jesus was set apart and commissioned for his task of saving humanity, and this also is the way in which his followers are set apart and commissioned for their mission in and to the world. Here is where we can see the classic and timeless model of discipleship, which involves close mentoring and preparation for the missional task, both on an individual and communal level.

3

Sanctification

The Age of the Spirit

Grounded in Jesus's teaching and within the framework of the early Christian mission narrated in Acts, the church takes its first steps in developing and maturing as a movement. In this early phase, we see a clear definition and consolidation of the gospel message, the establishment of local congregations, and an early emphasis on believers' need for holiness and sanctification. In this and the following three chapters, we will trace the teaching on sanctification in Acts, the New Testament letters, and Revelation in approximate chronological order (with some topical grouping) so as to get a sense of the organic development of the church's maturation and the New Testament teaching on sanctification. In this chapter, we make a start by looking at the account of the life of the early church in Acts, the letter of James, and Paul's letters to the Galatians and Thessalonians.

The Early Church

Acts provides an important nexus between the Gospels and the rest of the New Testament by recording the early church's mission starting in Jerusalem and reaching the ends of the Gentile world. Throughout Acts, we see the gospel progressing as the Spirit moves through the apostles' witness to the risen Jesus. In fact, Luke frames his narratives as the story of what Jesus continued to do in the power of the Spirit (Acts 1:1). Since many of the New Testament references to being holy are found in Acts, this book is pivotal for our understanding of sanctification. Paul is frequently shown in Acts as preaching to the Jews in the local synagogues and then moving on to the Gentiles after the Jews reject the message of the Messiah. Pentecost witnesses the transition from the old- to the new-covenant era (Acts 2), and the Jerusalem Council clears the way for Gentile inclusion in the new messianic community (Acts 15).

The outpouring of the Spirit marks the beginning of the age of the church. This new experience of the new covenant, worked out in believers' lives in Christ with the Spirit indwelling them, constitutes a new reality. As in the Gospels, if not more so, there is in Acts a strong *missional* component in sanctification. The literary structure of Acts presents the early, Spirit-empowered expansion of the church from its Jewish roots to a worldwide movement. The Acts narrative pointedly records salvation history as the work of God:

> Luke shows that the expansion of the gospel to the ends of the earth was a movement of God. Above all else, it was in obedience to and in fulfillment of the explicit command of Jesus (1:8). Each step happened with God's interested involvement. . . . The evangelization of Jerusalem came after the outpouring of the Spirit at Pentecost. In 8:4, the door was opened to Judea and Samaria. The persecution at the stoning of Stephen

and the subsequent Dispersion proved providential. Philip evangelized some Samaritans and then a Gentile God-fearer (the Ethiopian) at the command of an angel. . . . The outline of Acts is centered geographically: Jerusalem, Judea and Samaria, Asia Minor, Macedonia and Greece, and Rome. At the entrance of the gospel to each of these regions Luke was careful to note that the gospel penetrated these areas at the direction of God.[1]

At his final departure from a beloved church he established, Paul commends the Ephesian elders to God and his word, having preached the full counsel of God for three years. Warning them of impending dangers to come from within, as well as from the outside, Paul declares, "I commend you to God and to the word of his grace, which is able to build you up and to give you the inheritance among all those who are sanctified" (Acts 20:32). Paul's intense devotion to ministry amongst the Ephesians is evident in the many tears accompanying his departure. His last words to the Ephesian elders point them to the word of God as the "word of his grace, which is able to build you up and to give you the inheritance among all those who are sanctified." Many challenges lie ahead, yet the word and the Spirit will sustain them in their mission. This interchange is reminiscent of Jesus's prayer for, and commissioning of, his followers at the end of his earthly ministry. In view of their followers' anxiety at their departure, both Jesus and Paul point them to the word of God in order that they may be sanctified and sustained by its truth (cf. John 15:1–10).

Later, Paul reiterates the vital importance of sanctification in the contest of his appeal to the Roman emperor. Speaking to King

---

1. Andreas J. Köstenberger, L. Scott Kellum, and Charles L. Quarles, *The Cradle, the Cross, and the Crown: An Introduction to the New Testament*, 2nd ed. (Nashville, TN: B&H Academic, 2016), 431.

Agrippa, he tells the story of his conversion, recounting God's purpose for his life. He recalls the vision God gave him, "to appoint you as a servant and witness . . . to open their eyes, so that they may turn from darkness to light and from the power of Satan to God, that they may receive forgiveness of sins and a place among those who are sanctified by faith in me" (Acts 26:16–18). Agrippa sends Paul on to the next layer of Roman bureaucracy, telling him that his great learning has driven him insane. Yet at his trial, Paul testifies to the power and purpose of God for those who turn from darkness to light and are saved from Satan to receive the gift of forgiveness; these believers will have a place with God as those set apart for him, and kept for him, by faith in God.

The early church, and Paul in particular, provides us with inspiration for continuing in the mission of God. As God's people alive today, despite our human frailty and a plethora of obstacles, we must bring the message of salvation to unbelievers and instruct believers to be strengthened by the word in order to be sanctified and live lives devoted to God. The first-generation believers in Acts powerfully continued in the mission of God, preaching the forgiveness of sins and offering a place in God's kingdom to those who were sanctified by faith in Jesus:

> If the first generation of the Christian church proves anything, it is this: the power of God is infinitely greater than any human obstacles in its way. A humble Galilean craftsman, who suffered an untimely death and accumulated no earthly possessions, wrote no books, and left nothing behind but a small band of disheartened followers, spawned a movement so powerful that it took the Roman Empire by storm. . . . Luke's account of the spiritual exploits of the early church can serve as a mighty inspiration to the church of all ages,

which is faced with the same challenge of bearing witness to the living, resurrected Christ in a world hostile to the gospel message. As we continue this godly legacy, we must make sure our trust . . . is in the same God who raised Jesus from the dead . . . rather than in our own ability to overcome.[2]

Jewish Christianity

James is in all probability the earliest book of the New Testament, espousing for the most part a Christianized Old Testament ethic of living wisely and righteously. James is an exemplar of Jewish Christianity, with a focus on works that demonstrate the genuineness of a believer's profession of faith and an accompanying emphasis on decrying hypocrisy in the church. James starts out his letter as follows: "Count it all joy, my brothers, when you meet trials of various kinds, for you know that the testing of your faith produces steadfastness. And let steadfastness have its full effect, that you may be perfect and complete, lacking in nothing" (James 1:2–4). Here, James speaks about what being a perfect or spiritually mature person looks like. In particular, he mentions how suffering and various kinds of trials are means by which character is developed and steadfastness is revealed in a person's life. It is this steadfastness in the face of adversity that represents the proper response to the various challenges believers are sure to encounter. In this way, a person proves their maturity of character. Steadfastness in trials—that's perfection! According to James, people are complete and lacking nothing if they exhibit steadfastness under pressure.

From James's opening words, we can glean one particular goal or outcome of life in the Spirit. Of the many things on which James could have focused, he chose the characteristic of *steadfastness* amid

---

2. Köstenberger, Kellum, and Quarles, *Cradle, Cross, and Crown*, 397.

trials. Character is proven and demonstrated by how people respond to adversity. Will they remain consistent, unwavering, and resolute when confronting affliction? James does not speak much of the Spirit, but later we will discuss the role of the Spirit in producing spiritual fruit and effecting maturity. Endurance, therefore, ultimately reflects dependence on the work of the Spirit in a person's life. According to James, a person who bears up well under trials—and, in fact, considers them all joy—is "perfect" (*teleios*) and "complete" (*holoklēros*; cf. 1 Thess. 5:23), "lacking in nothing" (James 1:4). James's words here echo Jesus's teaching in the Sermon of the Mount: "Therefore be perfect, as your heavenly Father is perfect" (Matt. 5:48). While literal perfection is, of course, unattainable for sinful human beings on this side of heaven, proven character is not. Such spiritual maturity is the result of years of practice and the development of godly, righteous character.

Later in the book, James examines the evils of the tongue and comments on the serious responsibility of being a teacher, presumably because of the judgment that comes with the influence such a position inevitably entails. "Not many of you should become teachers, my brothers," James writes, "for you know that we who teach will be judged with greater strictness. For we all stumble in many ways. And if anyone does not stumble in what he says, he is a *perfect* man, able also to bridle his whole body" (James 3:1–2). One must guard one's tongue with particular care if serving as a teacher. In addition to steadfastness under trials, therefore, James tells us that *control of one's tongue* is a thermometer of a person's character. In believers' ability to control their speech, their ability to conduct themselves in other areas of life is revealed—they are able to control their entire body. So here we have a second characteristic by which to measure maturity: a person's ability to control his tongue.

Walking in the Spirit

Galatians is likely the next letter written in the New Testament. It is probably Paul's first epistle, sent to instruct the young church about basic doctrine and practice to be lived out differently now according to the new covenant. Serious adjustments were required of these new believers. The arrival of the Spirit entailed a new way of relating to God. Their previous way of life in the old-covenant era was no longer the norm, and believers faced opposition and misinformation regarding their new freedom in Christ. Paul, a converted Jew himself who had previously opposed Christianity, fully understood this contested yet basic truth: salvation is, and of necessity must be, a free gift given in Christ to be received by faith. As a result, Paul pointed to the law's limitations and its temporary function. Not that he considered the law itself to be deficient, but the misguided agitators in Galatia—the so-called Judaizers—who advocated continued dependence on Torah (law) observance for righteous living needed resolute correction.

In Galatians, Paul addresses believers' ongoing relationship with God and the sustenance of spiritual life in their relationship with God. In the new covenant, this relationship is sustained by the Spirit and no longer through animal sacrifices or law observance such as Sabbath-keeping, food laws, or circumcision. Prior to their new life in Christ, New Testament believers had not experienced the continual indwelling of the Spirit. It was at Pentecost that the Spirit came upon the first believers and the church was born (Acts 2). At this early stage in the history of Christianity, it is vital for believers to understand that the work of the Spirit in the life of born-again New Testament Christians is commensurate with the righteousness that is and has always been demanded by God. Thus life in Christ is to be lived according to the Spirit, not by observing mere external stipulations.

Against the backdrop of the Judaizing threat, Paul encourages the Galatian believers to continue in the Spirit. In support, he cites his own example: "I have been crucified with Christ. It is no longer I who live, but Christ who lives in me. And the life I now live in the flesh I live by faith in the Son of God, who loved me and gave himself for me" (Gal. 2:20). Paul no longer lives by his own strength but by faith in Jesus, the Son of God, who loved him and gave his life for him. This constitutes a powerful refutation of all moral self-effort in favor of the grateful reception of God's gracious redemption effected in and through the Lord Jesus Christ. In this context, Paul challenges those Galatian believers who are tempted to return to the old practices of the law in the strongest possible terms: "Are you so foolish? Having begun by the Spirit, are you now being perfected by the flesh? Did you suffer so many things in vain—if indeed it was in vain? Does he who supplies the Spirit to you and works miracles among you do so by works of the law, or by hearing with faith—just as Abraham 'believed God, and it was counted to him as righteousness'"? (3:3–6).

Paul's logic here is compelling. The apostle reminds the Galatians that they were saved by grace, not moral self-effort, or "works of the law." If salvation is by grace, sanctification must be by grace as well. They had received the Spirit by faith, not works. But if they began their new life in Christ by the Spirit, they must continue the way they started—by the Spirit. Perfection can never come "by the flesh"—that is, human self-effort consisting in religious works aimed at pleasing God. Paul adds three related points. First, if we can please God simply by performing certain religious rituals, why suffer (as apparently those young believers had already done)? Such suffering was the result of believers' association with the crucified Christ (cf. Gal. 2:20). Second, God had supplied his Spirit and worked miracles among them because they had heard the gospel and responded in faith, not in response to their moral self-effort. Third, Paul adduces a biblical example, Abraham the patriarch, who, as Scripture makes clear, was considered righteous by God on the basis of faith, not works (cf. Gen. 15:6; cf. Rom. 4:1–3, 22–25).

Paul's emphasis on the indispensable work of the Spirit in sanctification anticipates his even fuller treatment in Galatians 5, where Paul instructs the Galatians how to live in light of their newfound freedom in the Spirit—not to seek justification by law-abiding righteousness but to serve one another in love, in fulfillment of God's purposes through the Spirit: "For you were called to freedom, brothers. Only do not use your freedom as an opportunity for the flesh, but through love serve one another. For the whole law is fulfilled in one word: 'You shall love your neighbor as yourself.' But if you bite and devour one another, watch out that you are not consumed by one another" (5:13–15). If they lovingly serve one another in the freedom of the Spirit, these believers will fulfill "the whole law"!

But how are these believers to follow this instruction to use their freedom to love one another? Paul goes on to tell them to *walk by the Spirit*. They know—as we do—that they have the indwelling Spirit. To "walk by the Spirit" indicates a movement concurrent with and according to the influence and guidance of the Spirit. The Spirit should be leading our steps, inspiring our movement, and infusing our relationship with God in Christ. We may not know ahead of time which way we should go, but at each step we can be aware of the Spirit's guidance and then move in the direction he leads. This starts with a listening posture, a general openness to God's leading, and a preparedness to obey God's revealed will in Scripture, especially in the moral arena. Paul writes, "I say, walk by the Spirit, and you will not gratify the desires of the flesh. For the desires of the flesh are against the Spirit, and the desires of the Spirit are against the flesh, for these are opposed to each other, to keep you from doing the things you want to do" (Gal. 5:16–17).

In this way, as believers focus on the Spirit, they resolutely avoid the potential impact of the sinful nature that still dwells within them. Not that there are no other negative influences in their lives that will challenge them. The fallen world system revolves around self rather than Christ; evil supernatural forces will attack when believers least expect it. But as they learn to walk according to the Spirit, or to "keep in step with the Spirit" (cf. Gal. 5:13–25), they will grow in their ability to live in such a way that they glorify God amid the various afflictions they face. It is not that the flesh is obliterated; it is still present in their inner being and raises its ugly head. Thus they need to continually walk in the Spirit and crucify their old, sinful nature. This requires a deliberate focus on God's work and the Spirit's leading. It also involves presenting their lives to God, listening to his voice, and engaging in continual prayer for help and guidance. Regular and ongoing nurture from God's word is vital for sanctification and part of the process of being conformed to Christ. This growth into maturity takes place as a result of the Spirit's work as believers choose to walk by the Spirit.

Conversely, Paul states that those who walk according to the flesh will not inherit God's kingdom (Gal. 5:21; cf. 1 Cor. 6:9). This implies that those who do not take seriously the necessity of walking by the Spirit and instead allow the flesh to express itself as a regular pattern of deliberate and unconfessed sin are likely not even saved and thus not indwelt by the Spirit. True believers should not allow their fleshly impulses to lead and control them so that they engage consistently and habitually in sin. A sinful pattern of living and a fleshly identity stand in stark contrast to a spiritual character expressed in the ninefold fruit of the Spirit (Gal. 5:22–24). Believers are spiritual because they have trusted in Christ by the Spirit and characteristically respond to the Spirit's promptings within them.

The questions to ask ourselves, then, are these: Which dynamic characterizes our lives? As an overall expression of who we are, are we marked by our sinful nature or the Spirit? The presence of Christ's transforming work in our lives through the Spirit will be evident both to ourselves and others. Genuine believers should display clear and abundant evidence of the Spirit's work in their lives. As Paul explains:

> If you are *led* by the Spirit, you are not under the law. Now the works of the flesh are evident: sexual immorality, impurity, sensuality, idolatry, sorcery, enmity, strife, jealousy, fits of anger, rivalries, dissensions, divisions, envy, drunkenness, orgies, and things like these. I warn you, as I warned you before, that those who do such things will not inherit the kingdom of God. But the fruit of the Spirit is love, joy, peace, patience, kindness, goodness, faithfulness, gentleness, self-control; against such things there is no law. And those who belong to Christ Jesus have crucified the flesh with its passions and desires. If we *live* by the Spirit, let us also *keep in step* with the Spirit. (Gal. 5:18–25)

We will know that we are walking in the Spirit when we see the fruit of the Spirit exhibited in our lives and the deeds of the flesh begin to wane. Paul's words here show that the activity of the Spirit in believers' lives is instrumental in producing spiritual fruit. The Spirit's role consists in crucifying the flesh with its passions and desires and engaging in an inner battle against the flesh. As Douglas Moo points out, 3:3 ("Having begun by the Spirit, are you now being perfected by the flesh?") and 5:5 ("Through the Spirit, by faith, we . . . eagerly await for the hope of righteousness") serve as "rhetorical bookends to Paul's theological argument and appeal to the Galatians."[3] In order to experience the new life, walking in the Spirit is a vital necessity:

---

3. Douglas J. Moo, *Galatians*, Baker Exegetical Commentary on the New Testament (Grand Rapids, MI: Baker Academic, 2013), 35.

Paul's purpose is both to warn and to assure believers. He warns them that Christians find themselves in the midst of a continuing battle between these two powers (see esp. vv. 17, 21). But, more importantly, he assures believers that, because we are in Christ (v. 24), the Spirit is now the dominant power and provides the believer with victory over the flesh (vv. 16, 24) and release from any threat that the law may pose (vv. 18, 23b).[4]

Moo elaborates, "The Spirit whom Paul now celebrates as the power of the new life is nothing other than that Spirit whom the prophets predicted would take possession of God's people in the eschatological age, providing for that wholehearted obedience to the Lord that the law could not secure ('the promise of the Spirit' in 3:14; see, e.g., Jer. 31:31–34; Ezek. 36:24–28; Joel 2:28–32)."[5]

Walking in the Spirit, then, is connected to obedience in the Christian life and no longer associated with obedience to the law of Moses. Obedience to the "law of Christ"—the life of Christian freedom fueled by grace and love—is the new and better way by which believers "bear one another's burdens" (Gal. 6:2). Obedience and walking in the Spirit are vital for growing in godliness: "Obedience is not the *basis* for eternal life but the necessary *means* by which our new life, based on Christ and faith and mediated by the Spirit, will be confirmed and sealed on the last day."[6] Life in the Spirit, according to Galatians, is a life that is justified by faith in Christ and characteristically exhibits the supernatural fruit of righteousness.

Comprehensive Sanctification

Acts 17 records the planting of the church at Thessalonica during Paul's second missionary journey. Paul was able to establish these be-

---

4. Moo, *Galatians*, 35.
5. Moo, *Galatians*, 35.
6. Moo, *Galatians*, 36 (emphasis added).

lievers in the faith for only a few weeks because of major opposition that hastened his departure from the city. One of Paul's purposes for writing his letters to the Thessalonians was to encourage the church during times of persecution and to urge believers to live holy lives characterized by sexual purity. In these letters, the apostle contends that the Spirit is active both at conversion and throughout believers' lives (1 Thess. 1:5–6). He stresses the vital importance of the Spirit in sanctification (1 Thess. 4:8; 5:23; 2 Thess. 2:13) and observes that believers are set apart from their pagan neighbors and empowered to witness to Christ. In addition, the Spirit enables believers to refrain from sexual immorality and other vices.

Regarding sanctification, Paul writes, "Finally, then, brothers, we ask and urge you in the Lord Jesus, that as you received from us how you ought to walk and to please God, just as you are doing, that you do so more and more" (1 Thess. 4:1). In this statement, Paul reflects on previous instructions given to the Thessalonians about how to live and please God, expressing the hope that they would do so increasingly. He acknowledges that they are doing so already but wants to encourage them to do so even more. As in Galatians, the apostle uses language of *walking* with regard to how believers are to live and please God. This image points to an ongoing personal relationship with God and has deep roots in Old Testament terminology: Enoch (Gen. 5:24), Noah (Gen. 6:9), Isaac (Gen. 48:15), and many other exemplary Old Testament figures "walked" with God. Walking with God is not just a sporadic experience of gaining power from God for one's life but rather entails a process that involves deliberate initiative on our part and continual attention to God's leading.

A few verses later, Paul refers once again to the Spirit's crucial role in believers' pursuit of holiness and emphasizes that sanctification is the will of God for them. In a short span of seven verses, we find several instances of sanctification language, underscoring that this is one of the preeminent New Testament passages on this topic:

> You know what instructions we gave you through the Lord Jesus. *For this is the will of God, your sanctification*: that you abstain from sexual immorality; that each one of you know how to control his own body in holiness and honor, not in the passion of lust like the Gentiles who do not know God. . . . For God has not called us for impurity, but in holiness. Therefore whoever disregards this, disregards not man but God, who gives his Holy Spirit to you. (1 Thess. 4:2–8)

Here is a clear call for holiness that, if unheeded, ignores not only Paul's instruction but God's. Two things stand out: the importance of holiness for the life of the believer and the means of holiness given by God in the person of the Spirit. This emphasis on the work of the Spirit is consistent in the New Testament's instruction on holiness. "Walking" language, used here again, indicates the manner and means of spiritual growth by which believers are to progress. As those attentive and responsive to the Spirit's leading, the Thessalonians were to be self-controlled and act honorably. Paul's instructions here serve as a reminder that holiness and sanctification are that to which believers are urgently called. In addition, Paul's call to holiness here relates to the particular need for the Thessalonians to abstain from impurity, sexual immorality, and lust and to better understand what it means to be holy.

On the heels of this passage on sanctification, following instructions about the Lord's return and the coming day of judgment, Paul closes with a list of instructions for the believers at Thessalonica that once again includes a prominent reference to sanctification: "Now may the God of peace himself *sanctify* you completely, and may your whole spirit and soul and body be kept blameless at the coming of our Lord Jesus Christ. He who calls you is faithful; he will surely do it" (1 Thess. 5:23–24). This desire for completion is similar to Paul's later words to the Philippians: "I am sure of this, that he who began a good work in you will bring it to completion at the day of Jesus Christ" (Phil. 1:6; cf. 1 Cor. 10:13).

We register four observations. First, God's desire is for believers' *complete sanctification*. He does not want them to be partially holy and partially unholy; the end goal is comprehensive sanctification.[7] Second, the time at which this comprehensive sanctification will be complete is on *judgment day*. Then they will be perfected in holiness and see Jesus face-to-face (cf. Matt. 5:8; 1 John 3:2). Third, at the root, sanctification is God's work, not that of believers. It is hard to imagine Paul expressing this vital truth more forcefully: "May the God of peace himself sanctify you completely. . . . He who calls you is faithful; he will surely do it." Fourth, because it is God who does the work, our ultimate and complete sanctification is an *absolute certainty*. If our sanctification depended on us, it could not be accomplished. But because it is God's work, it will be done—because he is faithful. This truth is exceedingly comforting and reassuring.

In his second letter to the Thessalonians, Paul again instructs these believers on the topic of sanctification, writing, "We ought always to give thanks to God for you, brothers beloved by the Lord, because God chose you as the firstfruits to be saved, through *sanctification* by the Spirit and belief in the truth. To this he called you through our gospel, so that you may obtain the glory of our Lord Jesus Christ. So then, brothers, stand firm" (2:13–15). The sanctification Paul addresses in this passage entails God's gracious work of

7. See Gregg R. Allison, *Embodied: Living as Whole People in a Fractured World* (Grand Rapids: Baker, 2021), esp. chap. 7.

setting sinners free from bondage to their sinful nature by moving them to repent and believe the gospel.

Summary

In Acts, we witnessed the growth of the early church as the first Christians powerfully proclaimed Jesus's resurrection, and, as a result, those who put their trust in Christ were "sanctified," set apart for God and his holy use. In our study of sanctification in the early New Testament letters, we have seen the church emphasize the necessity of life in the Spirit. We looked first at the letter of James. In keeping with Old Testament ethics, James paints a portrait of the "perfect and complete" person who displays steadfastness under trials. Those who walk in holiness exhibit self-control, particularly in speech. Just as faith without works is dead, the holy people of God who have "receive[d] with meekness the implanted word" (James 1:21) must "be doers of the word, and not hearers only" (1:23).

Next, we investigated what is likely the first letter Paul wrote, the epistle to the Galatians. Paul himself has been crucified with Christ and is living by faith. He chastises the Galatians for relapsing into a kind of works righteousness due to pressure by the so-called Judaizers who insisted that Gentiles must be circumcised before being allowed to join the Christian community, when in fact they had received salvation through the Spirit by faith. In chapter 5, Paul calls on believers to "walk in the Spirit," to "live by the Spirit," and "to keep in step with the Spirit." As such, they are to cultivate the ninefold fruit of the Spirit.

In his letters to the Thessalonians, Paul urges believers to pursue sanctification more and more. In fact, he teaches that sanctification is God's will for them. This includes believers' resolve to abstain from all forms of sexual immorality. People often ask what God's will is for their lives. While specifics may at times prove elusive, we can be assured of one thing: God's will for us entails living pure and holy lives that are free from sexual immorality and empowered by the Spirit.

Over against moral laxness and works righteousness, these letters remind Christians today that those who have been justified by faith in Christ should demonstrate the genuineness of their faith by walking in the Spirit, which is itself a work of the Spirit. We may take our spiritual status for granted, drifting toward unholiness and missing the blessing of God in our lives. Or we may start out with a clear understanding of God's grace when we put our faith in Christ at conversion, only to subsequently slide back into a pattern of self-effort, trying to live the Christian life in our own strength. But Paul insists that if we started by grace, we must continue in grace. Not only justification but also sanctification comes by grace through faith. Believers need to continue to look to the Spirit as God's agent for wisdom, power, and enablement as they go through their daily lives and face various struggles and temptations. They cannot live the Christian life in their own strength, nor are they called to do so. Instead, they're called to walk in the Spirit and watch God produce the fruit of righteousness—holiness that goes beyond mere external compliance but flows from a regenerate heart.

4

Community

United to Christ

In Paul's correspondence with the Corinthians, the believers in Rome, and the church at Ephesus, we see the full flowering of Paul's teaching on life in the Spirit. Importantly, this teaching involves both *individual* and *corporate* aspects of sanctification. Paul's primary burden in this phase of his ministry is on the church's unity. His argument, as we will see, is that believers are "in Christ" by the *one* Spirit who indwells individual believers. Thus, individual indwelling by the Spirit forms the basis of the corporate unity of the church.

"In Christ" Language in Paul

Believers' holiness and sanctification are predicated upon their salvation and the union they have with Christ. There are many things in which they partake, or to which they are invited, because of their union with Christ. This participation is indicated by the many verses that feature the phrase "in Christ" and other similar phrases, such as "into Christ," "through Christ," and so forth.[1] The phrase "in Christ" occurs numerous times in the Pauline writings.[2] The New Testament associates union with Christ with specific character traits, actions, activities, and experiences. Some poignant examples of "in Christ" language related to sanctification in Paul's letters include the following:

> To the church of God that is in Corinth, to those sanctified *in Christ Jesus*, called to be saints together with all those who in every place call upon the name of our Lord Jesus Christ, both their Lord and ours. (1 Cor. 1:2)

> Therefore, if anyone is *in Christ*, he is a new creation. The old has passed away; behold, the new has come. All this is from God, who through Christ reconciled us to himself and gave us the ministry of reconciliation; that is, *in Christ* God was reconciling the world to himself, not counting their trespasses against them, and entrusting to us the message of reconciliation. (2 Cor. 5:17–19)

> Blessed be the God and Father of our Lord Jesus Christ, who has blessed us *in Christ* with every spiritual blessing in the heavenly places. (Eph. 1:3)

> Even when we were dead in our trespasses, [he] made us alive together with Christ—by grace you have been saved—and raised us up with him and seated us with him in the heavenly

---

1. See Constantine R. Campbell, *Paul and Union with Christ: An Exegetical and Theological Study* (Grand Rapids, MI: Zondervan, 2012), 420.
2. The use of "in Christ" language is not entirely unique to Paul in the New Testament. The phrase also occurs in Peter's writings. See, e.g., 1 Pet. 3:16: "Those who revile your good behavior *in Christ* may be put to shame"; 5:10: "the God of all grace, who has called you to his eternal glory *in Christ*, will himself restore, confirm, strengthen, and establish you"; and esp. 5:14: "Peace to all of you who are *in Christ*."

places *in Christ Jesus* so that in the coming ages he might show the immeasurable riches of his grace in kindness toward us *in Christ Jesus*. (Eph. 2:5–7)

For we are his workmanship, created *in Christ Jesus* for good works, which God prepared beforehand, that we should walk in them. (Eph. 2:10)

Now *in Christ Jesus* you who once were far off have been brought near by the blood of Christ. (Eph. 2:13)

Be kind to one another, tenderhearted, forgiving one another, as God *in Christ* forgave you. (Eph. 4:32)

The peace of God, which surpasses all understanding, will guard your hearts and your minds *in Christ Jesus*. (Phil. 4:7)

My God will supply every need of yours according to his riches in glory *in Christ Jesus*. (Phil. 4:19)

Formerly I was a blasphemer, persecutor, and insolent opponent. But I received mercy because I had acted ignorantly in unbelief, and the grace of our Lord overflowed for me with the faith and love that are *in Christ Jesus*. (1 Tim. 1:13–14)

Paul, an apostle of Christ Jesus by the will of God according to the promise of the life that is *in Christ Jesus* . . . (2 Tim. 1:1)

Do not be ashamed of the testimony about our Lord, nor of me his prisoner, but share in suffering for the gospel by the power of God, who saved us and called us to a holy calling, not because of our works but because of his own purpose and grace, which he gave us *in Christ Jesus* before the ages began. (2 Tim. 1:8–9)

I endure everything for the sake of the elect, that they also may obtain the salvation that is *in Christ Jesus* with eternal glory. (2 Tim. 2:10)

According to these passages, and others not cited above, *experiences* in which believers participate "in Christ" include (1) receiving redemption and justification by grace (Rom. 3:23–24); (2) receiving the Spirit, sanctification, and the calling to be saints (1 Cor. 1:2); (3) receiving various spiritual blessings (1 Cor. 1:4–9; Eph. 1:3); (4) freedom from the law (2 Cor. 3:14; Gal. 2:3–5); (5) being Christ's workmanship in order to do good works prepared beforehand (Eph. 2:10); (6) receiving salvation and being raised up with him and seated with him in the heavenly places ready to receive the immeasurable riches of his grace in the coming ages because of his kindness (Eph. 2:5–7); (7) becoming a new creation (2 Cor. 5:17); (8) being brought near to God (Eph. 2:13); (9) being forgiven as part of the kindness and tenderheartedness of God (Eph. 4:32); (10) being guarded by the peace of God that surpasses all understanding (Phil. 4:7); (11) having all needs provided (Phil. 4:19); (12) receiving the mercy and grace of our Lord that overflows with faith and love (1 Tim. 1:14); (13) receiving the promise of life (2 Tim. 1:1); (14) sharing in suffering for the gospel by the power of God, having been saved and given a holy calling (2 Tim. 1:8–9); and (15) obtaining salvation with eternal glory (2 Tim. 2:10).

Other verses use "in Christ" terminology in different ways, viewing it from slightly different angles to communicate distinctive nuances of the term.[3] These include asserting general *characteristics* of believers, their new *status*, and *benefits* received by those in Christ, along with other elements such as to signify Christian identity (i.e.,

---

3. Rom. 16:10; 1 Cor. 4:10; Phil. 1:26; 2:1–3; Col. 1:25b–29; 2 Tim. 1:13–14; 2:1–2; 3:12; Philem. 8.

being in Christ).[4] According to this set of passages, in Christ, believers are (1) approved (Rom. 16:10); (2) wise and strong (1 Cor. 4:10); (3) able to glory in him because of progress and joy in the faith related to Paul's or a mentor's influence (Phil. 1:26); (4) encouraged in him due to their participation in the Spirit, with affection and sympathy, being united and having the same disposition toward one another as Christ (Phil. 2:1–3); (5) presented mature as a result of the influence of the warning, proclamation, and teaching of Paul, a mentor, or leader (Col. 1:25b–29); (6) exhibit faith and love while following the pattern of sound words heard from Paul, a mentor, or leader (2 Tim. 1:13–14); (7) strengthened by grace in Christ and entrusted with the teaching of Paul, a mentor, or leader to pass biblical truths on to others who will in turn pass them on (2 Tim. 2:1–2); (8) live a godly life in him, with which comes persecution (2 Tim. 3:12); and (9) bold to command a follower regarding a requirement of faith but to do so in love (Philem. 8).

These blessings resulting from union with Christ express a fulfilling experience of unity and community. Each believer has the potential for progress and joy in affirming relationships with mature spiritual mentors while participating in Christ by the Spirit. Becoming wise through the correction, proclamation, and faithful teaching of church leaders and mentors, and following the pattern of faith exemplified by those who are in Christ, believers are trusted to pass on this privileged experience to others.

Called to Be Saints

Paul wrote 1 Corinthians to the church he planted at the thriving seaport of Corinth, most likely during his third missionary journey while being in the process of establishing the church in Ephesus. The

---

4. For an explanation of the grammar behind the different uses of "in Christ" terminology see Campbell, *Paul and Union with Christ*, chap. 3.

letter contains Paul's most extensive treatment of a variety of subjects such as Christian ethics, spiritual gifts, and believers' resurrection. It was written in response to a prior letter the Corinthians had sent to him with various queries (1 Cor. 7:1). Not only has he heard reports of general factional infighting (1:11) and divisions occurring even at the Lord's Supper (11:18); he has also become aware of a case of incest in the church (5:1), not to mention problems with the Corinthians' eschatology (chap. 15). Thus Paul writes 1 Corinthians to address these various concerns.

In 1 Corinthians Paul seeks to correct the Corinthians' misunderstanding as to how to grow spiritually. As David Garland suggests, "They may have understood the Spirit to be the inrush of heavenly power into their lives that granted them a new status and conferred upon them knowledge and great spiritual gifts. It could have fed their pride so that it grew to dangerous levels. They became 'puffed up' and 'arrogant' and fancied themselves to be 'spiritual ones' (3:1; cf. 2:13, 15; 9:11; 12:1; 14:37), 'mature' (2:6), and 'wise' (3:18; 4:10)."[5] He adds:

> Spiritual gifts apparently were compared and some were judged more or less spiritual and more or less valuable according to the same criteria employed in secular culture. . . . Paul will not address them as spiritual ones; they are instead fleshly (3:1), too much caught up in this world and its values. Everything occurring at Corinth proved his case: the power factions, the shocking case of incest, suing one another in pagan courts in order to get advantage over the other.[6]

Paul starts the letter as follows: "To the church of God that is in Corinth, to those *sanctified* in Christ Jesus, called to be *saints*

---

5. David E. Garland, *1 Corinthians*, Baker Exegetical Commentary on the New Testament (Grand Rapids, MI: Baker, 2003), 20.
6. Garland, *1 Corinthians*, 20.

together with all those who in every place call upon the name of our Lord Jesus Christ . . ." (1 Cor. 1:1–3). Little does the reader know at this point that not all is well. Before addressing a plethora of problems, Paul first notes that the believers at Corinth are *already* "sanctified," that is, set apart for Christ at conversion (*positional* sanctification). On the basis of this sovereign act of God, Paul affirms that they are "called to be saints": they are to *become* what they already *are* (*progressive* sanctification). Later, Paul affirms, "Because of him [God] you are in Christ Jesus, who became to us wisdom from God, righteousness and *sanctification* and redemption" (1:30). Jesus Christ *himself* is our sanctification, as well as wisdom from God, righteousness, and redemption. It is hard to overstate the significance of Paul's assertion here. Sanctification is not so much something believers *do*; it is *who Christ is*. As they are spiritually united to him, and in him with one another, and as the Spirit continually performs his sanctifying work in them, they grow in personal and communal holiness, being corporately set apart from the world and growing closer in their personal spiritual union with Christ in the Spirit.

This constitutes a powerful vision of God's sanctifying work, both individually and corporately. After a discussion of what it means to be spiritual in chapter 2, Paul laments:

> But I, brothers, could not address you as spiritual people, but as people of the flesh, as infants in Christ. I fed you with milk, not solid food, for you were not ready for it. And even now you are not yet ready, for you are still of the flesh. For while there is jealousy and strife among you, are you not of the flesh and behaving only in a human way? (1 Cor. 3:1–3)

In this passage, Paul identifies the Corinthians as spiritual infants. David Garland sheds light on why Paul would address them as "saints" yet still lament their lack of spirituality. According to Garland, "Spiritual persons are those in whom the Spirit has really become a fundamental power of life and who have 'the mind of Christ.' . . . As [those who are *sarkinoi*, fleshly], they are controlled by natural human impulses rather than the Spirit"; as weak and sinful believers, "they have not yet been freed from the normative practices of the world."[7] In fact, the conflict and divisions the Corinthians face may be due to the fact that they are fixated on certain styles of leadership. Many, it appears, favor the more eloquent approach of Apollos, preferring him to Paul. Others follow Peter, while yet others—one surmises those who consider themselves to be the most spiritual—profess to be followers of Christ himself! Yet while divisions in the church based on differing preferences with regard to people's oratory, personality, or leadership style were cause for concern, Paul discerns a deeper problem: "their failure to appreciate the incarnate message of the cross."[8]

Addressing a church where believers find great satisfaction in their spiritual giftedness, Paul paints a stark contrast between their self-perception and their true spiritual condition. In reality, the Corinthians are not spiritual but fleshly, holding "values, attitudes, and judgments, which manifest themselves in self-centeredness, self-indulgence, and arrogant self-sufficiency."[9] In fact, leaders such as Paul and Apollos each make a vital contribution; and they are all God's servants, and as his servants are dependent on him (1 Cor. 3:5–8).[10] The Corinthians' predicament highlights the problem of spiritual immaturity and worldliness among believers in the church. God expects believers to grow spiritually, yet there are some, or even many, whose growth is lagging behind. There is no necessary

---

7. Garland, *1 Corinthians*, 106.
8. Garland, *1 Corinthians*, 107.
9. Garland, *1 Corinthians*, 109.
10. Garland, *1 Corinthians*, 111.

correlation between a person's physical age and his or her spiritual maturity—even though there should be. Those of us who have been Christians for a number of years are expected to have grown spiritually in keeping with our spiritual age. Spiritual growth is not optional; it is expected.

Washed, Sanctified, and Justified

Despite their deficiencies, Paul still identifies the believers at Corinth as those "sanctified in Christ Jesus." He writes, "You were *washed*, you were *sanctified*, you were *justified* in the name of the Lord Jesus Christ and by the Spirit of our God" (1 Cor. 6:11). Garland observes that the epithet "holy ones" harks back to the Levitical code: "Speak to all the congregation of the people of Israel and say to them: You shall be holy for I the LORD your God am holy" (Lev. 19:2) and lists several implications for the Corinthian believers:

> First, they are "saints" by God's call (as Paul is an apostle by God's call). . . . Second, belonging to the holy people of God qualifies them as saints set apart to serve God's purposes, not their own. All Christians are equally holy so that none is to be regarded "saintlier" (in the modern sense) than others. Third, they are called to a particular lifestyle and are bound by moral strictures and standards of behavior because God is holy. . . . They are to embody values that are radically different from those in their surrounding culture. Fourth, the term "saints" has corporate significance. . . . They are not set apart from the world as lone saints but . . . as a community of saints with obligations to one another, as well as to God. . . . Paul wants this church to be whole and without divisions to represent God's holiness to the world.[11]

---

11. Garland, *1 Corinthians*, 27–28.

Paul also emphasizes Christian unity and believers' purity by linking both their individual bodies and the church with the Jewish temple. Correspondingly, the Spirit's presence fills both individual believers and the church as a whole. Just as God's Spirit filled the temple, God assigns great value to the individual believer's body and the corporate church as dwelling places of the Spirit. Anything that compromises the believer's purity or the church's unity is tantamount to destroying God's temple, an action which is sure to incur divine judgment.

New-Covenant Ministry

Paul's second letter to the Corinthians explains how the Holy Spirit is the agent of the new covenant. As such, the Spirit gives life with great and lasting glory to God but also as an effective means of transforming believers (2 Cor. 3). Contrasting life under the old covenant with life under the new covenant, Paul discusses how the Spirit in the new-covenant era works in the hearts of God's people. This, in turn, highlights the significance of Paul's new-covenant ministry to the Corinthians and beyond. Not only does the Spirit set people free; he also gives them life and transforms them from within, resulting in God's greater glory. In contrast to other leaders, Paul needs no letters of recommendation because the Corinthians themselves are his "letter of recommendation, written on our hearts, to be known and read by all" (3:2); they are "a letter from Christ delivered by us, written not with ink but with the Spirit of the living God, not on tablets of stone but on tablets of human hearts" (3:3).

Paul and his coworkers are "ministers of a new covenant, not of the letter but of the Spirit" (2 Cor. 3:6). If Moses's "ministry of death, carved in letters on stone, came with such glory that the Israelites could not gaze at Moses' face because of its glory, . . . will not the ministry of the Spirit have even more glory?" (3:7–8). When a person is converted to Christ, God removes the spiritual veil that previously kept him from seeing God's glory in Christ: "Now the Lord is the Spirit, and where the Spirit of the Lord is, there is freedom" (3:17). Paul concludes, "And we all, with unveiled face, beholding the glory of the Lord, are being *transformed* into the same image from one degree of glory to another. For this comes from the Lord who is *the Spirit*" (3:18). Paul's Spirit-related insights are as follows: "the Spirit operates on the human heart (v. 3); the Spirit gives life (v. 6); the Spirit conveys glory (v. 8); the Spirit imparts freedom (v. 17); and the Spirit effects spiritual transformation (v. 18)."[12] In all these ways, the apostle's ministry is superior to Moses and the law: "The law consisted of external regulations; law observance could not impart life; the giving of the law only resulted in veiled glory, which is reflected rather than lasting; the law could not effect true freedom from sin; and the law was unable to transform a person's inner being."[13] Sanctification in the new-covenant era—marked by freedom and grace—is empowered by the Spirit, who effects powerful and glorious spiritual transformation.

The Law's Limitations

Paul wrote Romans while planting churches at the end of his second missionary journey. The controversy over the necessity of Gentile converts' obedience to the Jewish law had been settled at the Jerusalem Council. Jewish-Gentile unity was now the central issue for Paul. In his preface, Paul asserts that the gospel he proclaims teaches justification by faith in Christ apart from works in keeping with Old Testament teaching (Rom. 1:1, 16–18). He is not ashamed of this gospel because it represents the power of God to save both Jews and non-Jews. Both groups are sinners (3:23) and justified

---

12. Gregg R. Allison and Andreas J. Köstenberger, *The Holy Spirit*, Theology for the People of God (Nashville, TN: B&H Academic, 2020), 135 (numbering removed).

13. Allison and Köstenberger, *Holy Spirit*, 135.

only by faith (3:26). This is in keeping with God's commendation of Abraham for his faith (chap. 4; cf. Gen. 15:6; Gal. 3). Abraham was justified by faith, and so are New Testament believers (Rom. 5:1–2). Just as in Adam all humanity sinned, so in Christ—the second Adam—all can receive life as a free gift (5:17). Paul's exposition of universal sin and the free gift of salvation through Jesus Christ concludes with a reference to the law: "Now the law came in to increase the trespass, but where sin increased, grace abounded all the more, so that, as sin reigned in death, grace also might reign through righteousness leading to eternal life through Jesus Christ our Lord" (5:20–21).

Why, then, does Paul return to the law in Romans 6 and 7 after having already demonstrated that believers are justified by grace through faith? It is hard to know; perhaps there were some in Rome who misrepresented Paul's teaching as antinomian (antilaw), or perhaps he wanted to address those in the audience—especially Jews—who were still not convinced that righteousness was unattainable by observing the law. In what follows, Paul uses a question-and-answer (diatribe) format to address the (limited) function of the law. The interpretation of chapters 6 and 7 is disputed. What is beyond dispute, however, is that the primary topic is the role of the law in the life of New Testament believers. In essence, Paul's argument is that the law must be set aside; in Christ, a different "law" had taken effect. This new law or principle was bound up with believers' identification with Christ in his death and resurrection—their union with Christ. As a result of their union with Christ, believers should present themselves to God rather than offer their members to sin as "instruments for unrighteousness" (6:13). Thus, sin will not reign in their mortal body; in Christ, believers have been set free from their bondage to sin as their new identity in Christ provides them with access to the powerful work of the Spirit.

United with Christ in his death and resurrection, believers can embark on a new way of life; sin no longer has dominion over them as it did prior to conversion. It is not that the sinful nature has lost all ability to influence believers; it remains part of them due to humanity's fall into sin. Even in Christ, believers do not immediately return to an Edenic state of perfection; this awaits their glorification. Yet the vital reality that has changed is that sin no longer has authority over believers. They can now offer themselves to God and his service, whereas previously, whether aware of it or not, they were presenting themselves to the service of sin and lawlessness. Correspondingly, Paul urges believers to offer themselves to the Lord in a spirit of humble submission and reliant trust. It follows that if believers are not living in one state—according to the Spirit—they are living in the other—the flesh. There is no spiritually neutral realm. In Christ, therefore, believers are not completely unaffected by the sinful nature but are free from its tyranny. They are now in Christ, and in him have the resources to overcome temptation and the oppressive power of sin.

What is more, living in Christ will effect a change in outcome in the believer's life. Whereas previously obedience to sin resulted in unrighteousness, now believers can choose to live in obedience to righteousness—presenting their bodies to its service—resulting in fruit leading to sanctification, that is, growth in holiness. The potential for obedience is there, but believers must still choose to offer themselves to God and live their lives for him. The once-for-all death of Jesus means that believers must consider themselves dead to sin and alive to God; they now have an orientation toward the things of God and are ready for his service, resulting in fruitful living. Having been saved, they have a wealth of resources at their disposal. In contrast to the refrain "Let go and let God," where one passively surrenders oneself to God so that he can do all the work, believers must be diligent and committed to do their part so that growth in godliness and effective witness can occur.

Indwelling Sin

In Romans 7, Paul examines how Christians are released from the law. Through no fault of its own, the law had the inevitable effect of exposing people's bondage to sin and their inability to live up to the law's righteous requirements. Believers have died to the law and thus no longer need to be held captive to it and the sinful passions it arouses in them. Though the law is holy and righteous, it magnifies the contrast between God's holy standard and sinful human beings apart from Christ. In this way, the law and sin join forces so as to expose sin for what it is when confronted with the righteous demands of the law. One key to understanding the argument in chapter 7 is to look to the concluding statement. Here we see that the above-mentioned struggle with sin is due to people's attempt to attain righteousness on their own apart from Christ. Yet it is only "through Jesus Christ our Lord" that our struggle with sin will ever come to an end: "Who will deliver me from this body of death? Thanks be to God through Jesus Christ our Lord!" (7:24–25).

Conversely, the struggle and defeat caused by sin described in Romans 7:13–25 echoes what the Old Testament reveals about Israel's failed attempts to live according to the covenant. Israel's failure pointed to the need for a perfect, righteous sacrifice for sin, which she was unable to offer in such a way that it could satisfy such a demand. The lesson to be learned from Israel's history is that people's struggle to overcome sin on their own apart from the provision made by Christ—in the power of the Spirit—will always result in ultimate defeat (cf. 9:30–33). In fact, trying to conquer sin on one's own will likely only intensify the struggle. While the Holy Spirit does not feature prominently in chapter 7, the principle of serving God in the new way of the Spirit is everywhere presupposed:

"But now we are released from the law, having died to that which held us captive, so that we serve in the new way of the Spirit and not in the old way of the written code" (7:6). It is in reliance on the Spirit that believers find relief from their perennial struggle with sin.

When Paul uses the first person singular ("I") in Romans 7:13–25, it is natural to assume he is speaking about himself. More likely, however, he is continuing to address generically a sinful person's inability to keep the law unaided by the Spirit. If so, rather than speaking about himself—whether before or after his conversion—Paul here employs a literary feature known as "rhetorical I" (cf., e.g., 1 Cor. 13:1–3). Thus, Paul uses a fictional character, a (Jewish) person who tries as hard as possible to keep the law but finds that the inherent sin nature is stronger.[14] In this case, the "I" designates neither Paul nor Adam nor Israel, but any individual who tries to obtain salvation through the law, delights in the law in his innermost being, and desires to obey God perfectly, but because of the sinful nature cannot do so. The clincher is that this person (the "I") does not in actuality exist. There is *no one* who fully delights in God's law in their inner being. Such a person is a mere rhetorical creation, not an actual historical person, serving to illustrate the dilemma faced by an individual, unable to live up to the demands of the law, who needs Christ to accomplish God's purpose of living a righteous life for his glory.[15]

Life in the Spirit

With this, we've arrived at the heart of our study of life in the Spirit. In fact, all of Romans 8 is essentially an exposé on this topic. The Christian life is to be lived apart from the law, based on the gracious

---

14. This might be labeled the "fictional illustration view." Andreas J. Köstenberger with Richard D. Patterson, *Invitation to Biblical Interpretation: Exploring the Hermeneutical Triad of History, Literature, and Theology*, 2nd ed. (Grand Rapids, MI: Kregel, 2020), 501.

15. See also the sample exegesis of Rom. 7:13–25 in Köstenberger with Patterson, *Invitation*, 496–501.

gift of Christ in the power of the Spirit. Instead of struggling to live according to the written code, believers now have the Spirit living inside them to guide them and to produce fruit in keeping with righteousness. Replacing the written law, "the law of the Spirit of life has set you free in Christ Jesus from the law of sin and death" (8:2), so that "the righteous requirement of the law might be fulfilled in us, who walk not according to the flesh but according to the Spirit" (8:4). This is indeed a momentous declaration: the "law of sin and death" has now been replaced by "the law of the Spirit of life," which has set believers "free in Christ Jesus." Jesus's work on the cross and the indwelling Holy Spirit thus enable believers to live righteous lives so that they can finally meet the "righteous requirement of the law," something they were unable to do prior to putting their faith in Christ.

We've already discussed believers' union with Christ—the fact that their new identity is now "in Christ" so that they can "walk in newness of life" (Rom. 6:4). In the present passage, however, there is a second important phrase that serves to describe believers' new identity: "in the Spirit" (8:9). Throughout this chapter, believers' lives are set in relation to the Spirit: they now operate on the basis of the "law of the Spirit of life" (8:2); they walk and live "according to the Spirit" (8:4, 5) and "set the[ir] mind on the Spirit" (8:6); they are "in the Spirit" who indwells them (8:9, 11); he is "the Spirit of Christ," and not having him means one is not a Christian (8:9). He is "the Spirit of him who raised Jesus from the dead"—the Spirit of God—who "will also give life" to our mortal bodies (8:11). He is the life-giving Spirit! What's more, "all who are led by the Spirit of God are sons of God" (8:14)— he is the "Spirit of adoption" by whom believers call God "Father" (8:15). And if children, they're also heirs—even "fellow heirs with Christ" (8:17). In this way, believers are taken into the intimacy of a family relationship with God the Father in his Son Jesus Christ through the Holy Spirit.

One important entailment of believers' familial relationship with God in the Spirit is eternal security, a doctrine affirmed throughout the New Testament. B. B. Warfield suggested that Paul here provides instructions regarding the spiritual and relational security of the believer in relation to God; it is the work of the Spirit in believers' lives that proves their sonship: "The leading of the Spirit thus appears constitutive of the sonship."[16] This further elucidates the connection between eternal security and Spirit-led living. While believers are given the choice of whether or not to live according to the Spirit—and must make this choice and actively pursue sanctification—those who are sons of God will in fact exercise this privilege as part of the outworking of their faith. Those who are not believers are depicted as living according to the flesh and in danger of failing to inherit salvation.

A Spirit-Filled Community

Paul's concern for the church's unity and believers' sanctification—a concern that pervades the book of Romans—continues to be a major theme in Ephesians. Paul wrote Ephesians most likely as a circular letter to churches in Asia Minor and vicinity during his first Roman imprisonment. In this letter, Paul expounds how God is at work to fulfill his perfect plan for humanity. God's dwelling amongst his people, which in ages past was manifested in the temple, now takes place in the context of "one body," as the indwelling presence of the Spirit builds believers together "into a temple in the Lord" (Eph. 2:16, 21).

We've already discussed the temple theme in the Old Testament and John's Gospel. Here, Paul speaks of believers growing "into a holy

---

16. Benjamin B. Warfield, *The Power of God unto Salvation: The Leading of the Spirit* (Grand Rapids, MI: Eerdmans, 1930), 154.

temple in the Lord" (Eph. 2:13–21), placing special emphasis on the peace that comes with membership in God's household. This peace is achieved by the agency of the Spirit. We have access to the Father through the Spirit, with Jesus as the centerpiece and foundation, the cornerstone by whom the entire building is held together. As a community of believers, we are now privileged to experience God's presence as we grow into this spiritual edifice—the church. This reality highlights the corporate dimension of sanctification that is so prominent in Paul's letters.

Paul also urges believers to be filled with the Spirit (Eph. 5:18).[17] Believers have been baptized into the Spirit upon regeneration and are already full of the Spirit. Why, then, does Paul urge them to be filled with the Spirit again? Ultimately, it is God's sovereign prerogative to fill believers with his Spirit as he chooses, at conversion and whenever he intends to empower them for special ministry or witness, to enable God-glorifying worship and God-honoring relationships. The command is often taken to imply that believers *must ask God* to fill them with the Spirit, a practice known as "spiritual breathing"—"expiring" or "breathing out" as one confesses and is cleansed from personal sin and carnality, and "inspiring" or "breathing in" as one takes in the Spirit by prayer once sin has been confessed and its influence upon a person is no longer overpowering. However, the instruction for believers to be filled with the Spirit is rather a command to *receive the filling of the Spirit at God's initiative.*

The corporate dimension of the passage is often overlooked, but note that the command to be filled is plural. Thus, Spirit-filling is more comprehensive than individual growth into maturity. The Spirit-filled community is made up of both believing Jews and

---

17. The scope of this volume does not permit a full treatment of this issue. For a thorough study of this passage and related issues, see Andreas J. Köstenberger, "What Does It Mean to Be Filled with the Holy Spirit?," *Journal of the Evangelical Theological Society* 40 (1997).

Gentiles. Not only do God's people constitute a "dwelling of God in the Spirit"—the new-covenant community as God's temple—we also reflect unity within diversity. It is in the genuineness of our unity as God's people that we're the "dwelling of God," and only in this way can we achieve true maturity—the fullness of Christ—as we function in holiness as a healthy, diverse community of God. Not only does functioning as the community of God entail understanding the nature of God's people as a spiritual temple, a holy community where God dwells and where diverse people are united and operate in tandem; it also involves the exercise of diverse, uniquely assigned, God-given *spiritual gifts*. The exercise of spiritual gifts, in turn, works alongside individual growth in character and godliness. It serves to further the growth of the church *corporately* as God's glory is reflected in the multiple expressions of spiritual gifts in the body that serve together in harmonious unity to advance his kingdom. In this way, each individual has a unique set of spiritual gifts, which are given and exercised for the common good.

Finally, we should be careful not to conflate the various ministries of the Spirit. Being *filled* with the Spirit is not the same as being *led by* or *keeping in step with* the Spirit. Though Spirit-filling is often seen in Scripture in the spiritual empowerment of God's servants at specific ministry occasions, in the present instance it refers primarily to being *controlled* by the Spirit. Being filled with the Spirit is also not the same as demonstrating the *fruit* of the Spirit, the development of godly characteristics as an expression of the Spirit's sanctifying work in the believer's life (cf. Gal. 5:22–23). All these are various means by which we experience the Spirit and grow in Christ, both individually and corporately.

Summary

In this chapter, we've taken a closer look at Paul's teaching on sanctification in his letters to the Corinthians, Romans, and Ephesians.

We examined the use of the phrase "in Christ" in Paul's writings. Because believers enjoy union with Christ, they participate in the life of Christ. Because Christ has made atonement for sins as their representative, Christians receive the benefits of his righteousness imputed to them. The Spirit is given by Christ to those for whom he died and who put their trust in him, while the indwelling Spirit communicates all his blessings to them. The positional sanctification that empowers progressive sanctification is first and foremost a participation in the life of Christ.

We saw that Paul addressed 1 Corinthians "to those sanctified in Christ Jesus, called to be saints together with all those who in every place call upon the name of our Lord Jesus Christ" (1:2). This opening address is particularly remarkable, as the Corinthians were far from being perfect. In fact, Paul spends much of the letter addressing various problems in the church, including immature views of leadership and the improper exercise of spiritual gifts. Nevertheless, Paul affirms at the very outset that Christ himself is both our righteousness and sanctification. Later, he urges the Corinthians to stay away from sexual immorality, reminding them, "You were washed, you were sanctified, you were justified in the name of the Lord Jesus Christ and by the Spirit of our God" (1 Cor. 6:11).[18] In 2 Corinthians Paul contrasts life under the old covenant with life under the new covenant, depicting the Spirit's ministry as one of glory, freedom, and inner transformation.

We also engaged in a study of Paul's teaching on sanctification in Romans, with special focus on chapters 6, 7, and 8. Highlights included our need to present our bodies to God as instruments of righteousness, which involves a deliberate, conscious choice to serve God in the power of the Spirit rather than succumb to our sinful

---

18. Interestingly, here "sanctified" is mentioned before "justified." This further underscores that "sanctified" is used here, as in 1:1, with reference to God's initial setting apart of people at the moment of conversion.

nature. We interpreted Paul's reference to the "wretched man" in Romans 7 as part of a fictional illustration by which Paul sought to demonstrate the impossibility of keeping the law perfectly no matter how hard a person may try to do so. This was shown to be part of a lengthy digression in chapters 6 and 7, aiming to clarify the limited efficacy of the law in view of our indwelling sin nature. The problem clearly is not with God's righteous standards but with our inability to keep them apart from the Spirit's enablement. In fact, self-effort only serves to intensify the struggle. The Spirit's work, for its part, is contingent on Christ's finished work on the cross, which means the role of the law has now been fulfilled. As a result, the law of new life in the Spirit has now taken its place. This shift is a crucial component of the New Testament teaching on sanctification.

Finally, we saw how Paul stressed the corporate dimension of sanctification in Ephesians. He depicts the church as a spiritual temple where both Jews and Gentiles are built together into a dwelling place for God by the Spirit. This theme was shown to find a continuation in Paul's command to "be filled with the Spirit," addressed to the church as a whole. In keeping with Old Testament temple imagery, Paul envisioned the church as the Spirit-filled "temple of God" where God-pleasing worship is rendered in the Spirit and through God-honoring relationships.

superior to the old (see, e.g., 2:1–4). The author encourages believers to live out their faith amid these challenges. Their resolve should come from the superiority of Jesus's ministry, as the author emphasizes "the unmatched, eternal high priesthood of Jesus Christ, the once-for-all character of his substitutionary sacrifice, and particularly the inauguration of the new covenant."[1] Now that Jesus had been crucified, risen from the dead, and "sat down at the right hand of the Majesty on high" (1:3), it was unthinkable that anyone could remain under the old-covenant system that had been rendered obsolete.

The entire message of Hebrews is tied up with God's climactic revelation and Christ's once-for-all work on the cross. While in the past God revealed himself through various prophets and in various ways, in these last days God has revealed himself *definitively* "by his son" (1:2). Jesus is superior to all previous servants of God, whether angels, the law, Moses, Joshua, or Aaron. He established the new covenant that had been announced by the Old Testament prophets (8:8–13, citing Jer. 31:31–34), rendering the old Mosaic covenant obsolete. In Jesus, God has provided a new and living way. Regarding this new way of life, the author of Hebrews shows that Jesus led the way in suffering and thus serves as an example for believers as they endure righteous suffering as part of their sanctification: "For it was fitting that he, for whom and by whom all things exist, in bringing many sons to glory, should make the founder of their salvation *perfect through suffering*. For he who *sanctifies* and those who are *sanctified* all have one source. That is why he is not ashamed to call them brothers, saying, 'I will tell of your name to my brothers; in the midst of the congregation I will sing your praise'" (2:10–12).

---

1. Andreas J. Köstenberger, L. Scott Kellum, and Charles L. Quarles, *The Cradle, the Cross, and the Crown: An Introduction to the New Testament*, 2nd ed. (Nashville, TN: B&H Academic, 2016), 762.

Mediator of a New and Better Covenant

While the author alludes to Jesus's priestly role at the very outset (Heb. 1:3), it is at 4:14 that he turns his full attention to this topic:

> *Since then we have a great high priest* who has passed through the heavens, Jesus, the Son of God, let us hold fast our confession. For we do not have a high priest who is unable to sympathize with our weaknesses, but one who in every respect has been tempted as we are, yet without sin. Let us then with confidence draw near to the throne of grace, that we may receive mercy and find grace to help in time of need.

In what follows, the author first explains the role of such a high priest in general (Heb. 5:1–4), then proceeds to introduce the idea of Jesus's priesthood being unique in that it does not follow the Levitical line but is patterned after Melchizedek (5:10). After a digression, the author returns to the topic at 6:20 and then elaborates upon Jesus's eternal high priesthood at great length in chapter 7. Understanding Jesus's high priesthood is critical if we are to grasp the shift from the old to the new covenant with regard to sin: under the former, the sacrificial system accounted for sins and provided temporary forgiveness, but under the latter, the forgiveness of sins is permanently effected in Christ. The role of Jesus as abiding high priest points to the eternal and permanent nature of Jesus's priesthood according to the order of Melchizedek and identifies Jesus as the mediator of a new and better covenant that definitively supersedes the old:

> Jesus is indeed a priest—yet one of a higher order, following not the Levitical pattern but that of Melchizedek. This, in turn, follows plainly, as he goes to great pains to show— from OT teaching, namely the references to Melchizedek in Genesis and Psalm 110. In fact, the latter passage already

states that Melchizedek's priesthood is eternal. . . . The author enjoins his readers to place their faith in Jesus—not only as the Messiah and Son of God but also as the eternal high priest whose ministry far exceeds that of the Levites with their tedious, repeated sacrificial offerings. . . . The entire OT sacrificial system is now rendered obsolete.[2]

What the Levitical priesthood lacked in its inability to forgive sins permanently, Jesus provided by the one-time, perfect sacrifice of himself. Thus, Jesus can "utterly" save those who draw near to him since he continually exercises his priesthood and intercedes for them in his high-priestly, mediatorial role. There is no longer any need to appoint new priests to replace those who die; nor is there any more need for recurring sacrifices. The perfect sacrifice Jesus offered is enough to cover all sins forever.[3] The Levitical priesthood was an important means by which God upheld the standard of righteousness for his people Israel during Old Testament times; yet its function was temporary. Rather than providing permanent forgiveness, it pointed to the necessity of a future means of lasting forgiveness through the substitutionary sacrifice of the eternal high priest, the Lord Jesus Christ. Hebrews teaches that in the Old Testament, cleansing was necessary to serve God, but, as David Peterson explains, the sacrifices did not satisfy the need for the permanent cleansing of one's conscience:

> The purpose of ritual cleansing in the Old Testament was that the people might be consecrated again to God's service. But the worshippers could not be perfected with respect to their consciences (9:9) and so they were sanctified only in a

---

2. Andreas J. Köstenberger, *Handbook on Hebrews through Revelation* (Grand Rapids, MI: Baker, 2020), 31–32.

3. See also the Old Testament discussion on this in chap. 2.

limited way (9:13). The New Covenant promise of a renewed "heart" is fulfilled when people are set free from the burden of unforgiven sins through trusting in the effectiveness of Christ's sacrifice (9:14; 10:22). They are thus renewed in faith and sincerity toward God. Only the cleansing provided by Christ can definitively free us to worship or serve the living God (9:14) in a way that pleases and truly honors him.[4]

A New and Living Way

Because of Jesus's effectual sacrifice, believers can now draw near to God "with a true heart in full assurance of faith," having been "purified" and sanctified positionally (Heb. 10:22). Justified by Christ and by virtue of their positional sanctification, believers have been launched on the path toward progressive sanctification. They have open access to God by which they can grow in Christlikeness, whereas before they did not. Since they have received permanent forgiveness through Jesus's once-for-all sacrifice for sins, they are to accept and live out this forgiveness and pursue purity by faith. There is no reason to continue living in sin. If anyone lives in the knowledge of Jesus's sacrifice yet continues to sin, there no longer remains any further sacrifice (cf. 2:1–3; 6:4–6). At the same time, believers still need renewal and cleansing and have been given access to God's provision toward that end. They can now draw near to him with confidence (4:16; 10:22).

There is a *new and living way* that has been provided for believers—new and direct access to God—through Jesus the great high priest (Heb. 10:20). The ensuing instruction, then, is for believers to spur one another on to love and good works (10:24). This indicates their continuing need for encouragement to spiritual activity

---

4. David Peterson, *Possessed by God: A New Testament Theology of Sanctification and Holiness*, New Studies in Biblical Theology (Downers Grove, IL: IVP Academic, 1995), 39.

and growth. In response to the initial positional sanctification they have been given, they are called to put their faith into corresponding action. If fearful judgment awaits those who continue in deliberate sin, it is clear that believers should take seriously their responsibility to engage in good works. This is not to be done in a legalistic fashion, however. Since believers now have new access to God's empowering presence, righteous activities should flow from their redeemed hearts, energized by the indwelling Spirit. This is the ongoing dimension of sanctification. For those who continue in the habit of sinning, a "fearful expectation of judgment" awaits (10:27). Most likely, those who continue in sin were never true, regenerate believers in the first place.

The Great Hall of Faith

In the remainder of the letter, the author stresses the vital importance of continual faith for those who strive to be perfected and completed in Christ. This faith is evidenced in those included in Hebrews 11, a section of the letter commonly called the "Great Hall of Faith," waiting for the heavenly city to be prepared for them. The author cites numerous Old Testament examples for believers to follow, most notably Abraham and Moses (11:8–12, 17–28). Though these forebears of the faith had not yet received the fulfillment of God's promises, they clung to the promise *by faith* that God would one day fulfill his promises to them and make them perfect (11:13–16, 39–40). That said, Jesus is the ultimate example for believers, as well as the one who enables them to have faith in the first place. In fact, he is the "perfecter of the faith," having completed his high priestly work: "Therefore, since we are surrounded by so great a cloud of witnesses, let us also lay aside every weight, and sin which clings so closely, and let us run with endurance the race that is set before us, looking to *Jesus, the founder and perfecter of our faith*, who for the joy that was set before him endured the cross, despising the shame, and is seated at the right hand of the throne of God" (12:1–2; cf. 1:3).

In view of Christ's finished work, the author encourages believers not to give up, reminding them of how Jesus himself endured great opposition from sinners (Heb. 12:3–4). In view of the threat of persecution and the temptation to return to their previous way of life in Judaism, believers are urged to persevere in their faith. In addition, the author indicates that there is a lack of maturity amongst the believers he addresses. Thus, he sets out to encourage them in their solidarity with those of great faith who preceded them. Reminding these immature believers of their faithful heritage provides them with real-life examples to emulate. Believers are also instructed to accept an important means of growth and refinement toward maturity in their lives: *God's discipline*. As the original readers experienced constant pressure to abandon their new way of life in Christ, believers today may be tempted to give in and succumb to temptation. Along with the Hebrews, they are encouraged to see God's discipline as a vital tool for their good and growth in Christ (12:3–14). God disciplines his people so that they may increasingly share in his holiness. In love, God treats them like children whom he wants to train in holiness through fatherly discipline.

The author then compares life under the old covenant with life under the new, contrasting them by comparing them respectively to Mount Sinai—where Israel received the law—and Mount Zion, the eschatological mountain of God. The old covenant had terrifying manifestations (see Heb. 12:18–21), which are well known from the exodus narrative, whereas the new covenant is bound up with celebrations amongst a host of angels and the saints who have been made perfect by Jesus, the mediator. The latter is the infinitely better, more effective way. In Christ, believers are no longer bound and burdened by an ineffective religious system and set of regulations.

Sanctification, Suffering, and God-Pleasing Sacrifices

We learn more about sanctification from the way Jesus suffered, which we are to emulate. We've seen that "it was fitting that he, for whom and by whom all things exist, in bringing many sons to glory, should make the founder of their salvation perfect through suffering. For he who sanctifies and those who are sanctified all have one source" (Heb. 2:10–12). Now, as he comes to end of his letter, the author issues several exhortations in view of the fact that Jesus's suffering took place outside the gate "in order to sanctify the people through his own blood." Correspondingly, believers are to "go to him outside the camp and bear the reproach he endured" (13:13; cf. 10:33; 11:26; 13:13).

Suffering is inevitable in the life of the Christian. The author indicates that in God's sovereign providence, suffering serves as an important means for believers' sanctification. As they follow the crucified Christ, as God's emissaries living set-apart lives they will inevitably encounter criticism, discrimination, outright persecution, or even martyrdom. While we are not to seek out suffering for the purpose of growth, we should be ready for it and even expect it. Sooner or later, committed believers will suffer. The connection with Christ and his suffering is an inescapable corollary of believers' identification with their crucified Savior.

Finally, the author instructs his readers as to what compares with Old Testament sacrifices. The sacrifices followers of Christ are to offer no longer serve the purpose of procuring temporary forgiveness and cleansing from sin as in the Old Testament. This cleansing and forgiveness have been accomplished once and for all through Jesus's death on the cross. What remains for us to do is live out our sanctification in keeping with our newfound relationship with the God who saved us. Such "sacrifice[s] of praise" offered to God involve presenting our very lives to him, offering up to him all that we do in the form of good works and generosity for the sake of his name and in his name (Heb. 13:15). This includes following Christ and identifying with him boldly and steadfastly, enduring in our faith through the various challenges that are sure to come, and being unashamed of the gospel.

Call to Holiness

Peter wrote 1 Peter from Rome to warn believers regarding impending persecution. Animosity toward Christianity had been brewing in the empire's capital. Peter, writing from Rome, sees a "fiery trial" on the horizon and surmises it is just a matter of time before persecution and suffering will spread to the outskirts of the empire. He sets out to warn his readers that suffering lies ahead and seeks to equip them to fight the temptations that will accompany it. Chief among Peter's strategies for equipping these Gentile believers is a reminder of their distinct identity as the people of God—their positional holiness and the corresponding call to progressive holiness. As Peter Walker explains, "An integral part of the author's purposes is to encourage his readers that, even though they might consider themselves as 'exiles of the Dispersion' (1:1), living in the province of Asia Minor and at some distance from Jerusalem, nevertheless they are at the center of God's purposes. Although previously they were 'not God's people,' now they are (2:10). Jesus' death and resurrection had occurred far away in Jerusalem ('Zion': 2:6), but these events had been expressly for their benefit."[5] Walker adds:

> As part of this pastoral strategy, Peter develops a new understanding of Jerusalem and its Temple. . . . These Christians

---

5. Peter W. L. Walker, *Jesus and the Holy City: New Testament Perspectives on Jerusalem* (Grand Rapids, MI: Eerdmans, 1996), 309–10.

must consider themselves as a new Temple. There was no need for them to make a pilgrim visit to Jerusalem's Temple or to confirm their status as "proselytes," because the important thing was to "come" to Christ, . . . who as a "*living stone*" was not tied to any one place. Indeed through their integral relationship with the Risen Christ, they themselves now constituted a "spiritual house" and a "holy priesthood" (2:5)—metaphors quite clearly taken from the Jerusalem Temple, . . . "offering spiritual sacrifices" which would be "acceptable to God." All the blessings and spiritual import that had previously been localized in the Jerusalem Temple were now theirs in Christ.[6]

Peter's logic in 1 Peter 1:1–7 can be summed up as follows:

In life, we will face trials; nevertheless, we should remember *who* we are and *what* we exist for. We are not our own if we are in Christ. He has bought us with a price. We exist to bring glory to God by growing in [our] life that is devoted entirely to God. In Christ, we are sons of God. We have been transformed. God is the one who transforms us to be devoted to Him. . . . We can only be devoted to God because of Christ. And Christ can only accomplish this for us because of at least three important truths. First, Jesus was a lamb without blemish or defect who was slain for us. Second, Jesus was chosen for this before the creation of the world. Third, Jesus redeems us not with silver or gold but with his own blood.[7]

---

6. Walker, *Jesus and the Holy City*, 310.

7. Benjamin Montoya, "A Brief Book Summary from Books at a Glance: *Devoted to God: Blueprints for Sanctification* by Sinclair Ferguson," Books at a Glance, October 26, 2017, https://www.booksataglance.com/.

New Identity

Peter instructs these believers to live out their new identity as the people of God. He urges them to live "with fear throughout the time of [their] exile" (1 Pet. 1:17) and speaks of the "futile ways inherited from [their] forefathers" (1:18). He calls on them to keep their "conduct among the Gentiles honorable" (2:12; cf. 4:3)—which is remarkable since they are in fact Gentiles! Yet Peter contends that, spiritually speaking, they are no longer Gentiles but, now that they have turned from worshiping idols to Christ, have assumed a new identity: while they formerly were not a people, now they are the people of God (2:10). In keeping with Israel's calling, Peter calls his readers "a chosen race, a royal priesthood, a holy nation, a people for his own possession, that you may proclaim the excellencies of him who called you out of darkness into his marvelous light" (2:9–10). People's changed status should issue in their proclamation of God's excellencies.

Also, Peter reminds his readers that their life on earth is merely a temporary sojourn. They are to recognize and remember that this earth is only a temporary home. By calling his readers "elect exiles" and "sojourners and exiles" (1 Pet. 2:11; cf. 1:1), Peter makes clear that they are only resident aliens; thus, believers ought to keep set apart from the world and live holy lives. *Resident alien* is a term that captures a vital truth in the life of the Christian. Like visitors from another country, they sojourn for a time in a place that is not their own. Christians should recognize that though this worldly existence has value, it is only temporary. What is of value is what they can build and reap for their eternal home. They should therefore focus on eternal pursuits and aim not to be distracted by worldly quests. This eternal pursuit entails growth in personal godliness—sanctification. In so doing, believers return to God, the "Shepherd and Overseer of [our] souls," just like Jesus modeled for them:

He committed no sin, neither was deceit found in his mouth. When he was reviled, he did not revile in return; when he suffered, he did not threaten, but continued entrusting himself to him who judges justly. He himself bore our sins in his body on the tree, that we might *die to sin and live to righteousness.* By his wounds you have been healed. For you were straying like sheep but have now returned to the Shepherd and Overseer of your souls. (1 Pet. 2:22–25; cf. Isa. 52:13–53:12; see also 1 Pet. 3:18; 4:1)

Holy Women

Peter then addresses the situation—not uncommon in the first century—where Christian wives are married to unbelieving husbands. He calls on these wives to submit to their husbands, "so that even if some do not obey the word, they may be won without a word by the conduct of their wives, when they see your respectful and pure conduct" (1 Pet. 3:1–2). Notice the word play here between not obeying the word and being won without a word. Also, we see here the powerful testimony borne by the "respectful and pure conduct" of wives who submit to unbelieving husbands (though, of course, there is no command here for women to remain in dangerous situations). Peter goes on to paint a picture (similar to Paul in 1 Tim. 2:9–11) of women cultivating a "gentle and quiet spirit, which in God's sight is very precious" (1 Pet. 3:4), a deliberate contrast between what is of great worth in God's eyes and what worldly women prize: "the braiding of hair and the putting on of gold jewelry, or the clothing you wear" (3:3). This does not mean women should neglect their outward appearance or forsake all adornment, but it does speak to proper spiritual priorities. Peter goes on to present Abraham's wife Sarah as an example of how Old Testament "holy women who hoped in God used to adorn themselves, by submitting to their own husbands" (3:5–6).

Husbands, for their part, are called to show honor to their wives "as the weaker vessel" since they are fellow heirs of grace and to live with them "in an understanding way" so that their prayers may not be hindered (1 Pet. 3:7). This shows how holiness and sanctification are vitally important in marriages for both spouses. If husbands are harsh toward their wives or wives unsubmissive to their husbands, this discord will hinder their access to God. The common denominator here is mutual respect and honor, as spouses are brothers and sisters in the Lord and together will inherit salvation. Sanctification requires the cultivation of Christian virtues that are diametrically opposed to what is valued in the world, and this is no less true in the marriage relationship.

Summary

In the present chapter we continued our study of the New Testament teaching on sanctification with a study of books that deal significantly with suffering, namely Hebrews and 1 Peter. The letter to the Hebrews proved to be a rich treasure trove on sanctification. In fact, virtually the entire book is devoted to this subject. The author presents Jesus as the eternal high priest who through his once-for-all sacrifice opened access to God and his holiness for all who trust in him. The author also contrasts the old- and new-covenant systems, arguing compellingly for the superiority of the latter over the former. Believers must not neglect Christ's provision by reverting to the old covenant but rather approach God's throne through Christ with confidence and even boldness. This exhortation is especially relevant for Jewish converts who were accustomed to observing the law for righteous living. Jesus serves as both the author and perfecter of faith and as the forerunner who has already entered heaven, the perfect sanctuary. We can also look to a cloud of witnesses who have already run the race of faith with endurance and have gone ahead of us. Their examples should encourage us to resist in our struggle against sin and to withstand, if necessary, even persecution. In fact, suffering may serve as a purifying tool in God's hands, and believers should not despise the Lord's discipline.

Peter, for his part, focuses on believers' identity as resident aliens in this world. He urges them to be spiritually set apart, quoting Leviticus where God says, "Be holy, for I am holy." Peter goes on to affirm that believers are "living stones" in God's spiritual temple who are chosen and precious in the sight of God, a "spiritual house" and a "holy priesthood." Peter also applies God's call for holiness to the marriage relationship. He calls on wives to submit even to unbelieving husbands and to cultivate a gentle and quiet spirit, just as Sarah, an honorable, holy woman of the past, submitted to her husband Abraham. Husbands, in turn, are called to honor their wives as fellow heirs of grace.

6

Legacy

Love and Virtue

With this, we turn to the final phase in New Testament revelation. We have now reached the stage of further development and even legacy, a time when the transition from the apostolic to the postapostolic period is rapidly approaching. Both Paul and Peter will face martyrdom and write their final testaments to their churches and apostolic delegates. Paul stipulates qualifications for church leadership; both urge their followers to pursue Christian virtues and growth in godliness. Jude calls on believers to contend for the faith, while John, in his letters, extols the supremacy of love. Revelation, finally, records John's visions of the end of human history. During this period, sanctification continues to be a paramount concern, even if the topic is in some cases transposed into a different key.

Paul's Legacy: Instructions for Holy Living

We start this chapter by concluding our survey of Paul's teaching on sanctification. Toward the end of his ministry, Paul wrote three letters to his apostolic delegates Timothy and Titus. These letters are in some respects different from Paul's previous letters in that they are written not to entire congregations but to key church leaders. What is implicit throughout, and often made explicit as well, is that these leaders are called to set the example for other believers to follow in their Christian faith. This individual pursuit of godliness on the part of apostolic delegates such as Timothy and Titus, in turn, is set within the context of conceiving of the church as "God's household" (1 Tim. 3:15). As believers, we have become part of a new family, the family of God, united by our common faith in the Lord Jesus Christ. Just as in a natural household, in the church there are "parents"—fathers and mothers who are more mature and experienced in the faith— as well as younger men and women who relate to each other as brothers and sisters in God's household, their spiritual family in Christ.

Within the framework of the household metaphor, Paul addresses himself specifically to men and women in the church. Regarding men, he says, "I desire, then, that in every place the men should pray, lifting *holy* hands without anger or quarreling" (1 Tim. 2:8). Men, and particularly male leaders, should exhibit holiness in united prayer that is free from any anger or arguments. Regarding women, Paul writes:

> Likewise also . . . women should adorn themselves in respectable apparel, with modesty and self-control, not with braided hair and gold or pearls or costly attire, but with what is proper for women who profess godliness—with good works. Let a woman learn quietly with all submissiveness. (1 Tim. 2:9–11)

Paul's instructions for women here are that they clothe themselves modestly, no doubt in part not to tempt men by the way they dress, but also to avoid being ostentatious, imitating the ways of the world, where women seek to draw attention to their outward features. Instead, Christian women should exhibit self-control and pursue godliness that is manifested in good works. They also should display a humble demeanor and be teachable.[1]

As mentioned, Paul regularly instructs his apostolic delegates to set an example for other believers in the way they live. One passage that is particularly instructive with regard to sanctification is 2 Timothy 2:22: "So *flee* youthful passions and *pursue* righteousness, faith, love, and peace, along with those who call on the Lord from a *pure heart.*" As believers, therefore, we're called both to "flee" and to "pursue." Negatively, we are to actively distance ourselves from unwholesome influences and activities; positively, we are to chase after Christian virtues such as righteousness, faith, love, and peace. Notably, we are to do so not in isolation but *along with those who call on the Lord from a pure heart*—in community. This call necessitates mentoring and accountability in the local church.

In his letter to Titus, Paul makes clear at the very outset that the island of Crete, where Titus served, was a very immoral place: "One of the Cretans, a prophet of their own, said, 'Cretans are always liars, evil beasts, lazy gluttons.' This testimony is true" (1:12–13). These are harsh words, but they show that mature believers—and younger believers as well—are to be set apart from their worldly surroundings and be markedly different. Within the context of God's household, Paul writes to Titus about mentoring relationships between mature and younger believers. He first addresses Titus and tells him how to instruct older and younger men in the church, setting the example; on top of his list is self-control, which in many ways emerges as the cardinal, all-encompassing virtue in Paul's letters to Timothy and Titus (2:1–2, 6–8).

---

1. Peter's instructions in his first letter are entirely in keeping with Paul's instructions here (cf. 1 Pet. 3:1–6).

In between, he turns to women in the church at Crete. Just as in a natural household, mothers are to take their daughters under their wings and teach them about virtue, relationships, and life skills, so mature Christian women in the body of Christ are to mentor those who are younger and less experienced in the faith:

> Older women likewise are to be reverent in behavior, not slanderers or slaves to much wine. They are to teach what is good, and so train the young women to love their husbands and children, to be self-controlled, pure, working at home, kind, and submissive to their own husbands, that the word of God may not be reviled. (Titus 2:3–5)

In contrast to the surrounding impure Cretan culture, older women are to be "reverent," that is, God-fearing. They are to control their words ("not slanderers") and appetites ("slaves to much wine"). Undergirded by godly character, they are to "teach what is good" and so mentor the young women (*mentor* in the Greek means "instilling good sense and sound judgment"). We also see that sanctification plays out in marriages and families in the way women treat their husband and children. Not only are wives and mothers to love their husband and children; they are to be self-controlled, pure (cf. Titus 1:15), working at home, kind, and submissive—not only to be a blessing to them but also in honor of God's word. As we've seen throughout Paul's teaching, the call to holiness is manifested in definite expectations for the believer's varied relationships.

Jude's Legacy: Contending for the Faith

Like James, Jude was a half-brother of Jesus and thus part of his natural family (cf. Matt. 13:55). The exact date of Jude's letter is unknown, but because of 2 Peter's likely dependence on Jude—2 Peter 2 exhibits considerable overlap with Jude's letter—most believe Jude was written sometime in the 50s or early 60s AD prior to 2 Peter. For this reason we'll first discuss Jude and then move on to 2 Peter. Jude opens his letter by addressing himself "to those who are called, beloved in God the Father and kept for Jesus Christ" (Jude 1). He goes on to state his purpose as "appealing to you to contend for the faith that was once for all delivered to the *saints*" over against "ungodly people, who pervert the grace of our God into sensuality and deny our only master and Lord, Jesus Christ" (3–4). As believers, we're called, beloved, and kept for Jesus. As such, we have an obligation to defend the unchanging Christian faith against those who may claim to be Christians but practice a form of cheap grace. Anyone who truly appreciates God's grace in Christ and thankfully accepts his salvation by faith will be motivated to live a holy life rather than invoking grace in order to rationalize a sinful lifestyle. But, sadly, this is in fact what some so-called Christians are in the habit of doing—both then and now.

Jude's encouragement for true believers is this: "But you, beloved, building yourselves up in your *most holy* faith and praying in the Holy Spirit, keep yourselves in the love of God, waiting for the mercy of our Lord Jesus Christ that leads to eternal life" (Jude 20–21). In addition, believers should "have mercy on those who doubt" and try to "save others by snatching them out of the fire." While so doing, they should abhor sin so much that they "[hate] even the garment stained by the flesh" (22–23). Jude ends his letter with the beautiful notion that God is able to keep believers from stumbling and to present them "blameless before the presence of his glory with great joy" (24). Both in the present and in the future, therefore, we can count on God's enabling power to keep us close to him, to preserve us in holiness, and to one day present us blameless in his presence. As we've seen time and again, holy living is both a serious command of God and a promised work of his grace.

Peter's Legacy: Growing in Christian Virtues

Peter wrote 2 Peter at the end of his life as a sort of final testament or reminder (cf. 2 Pet. 3:1). According to church tradition, Peter was martyred under Nero soon after writing 2 Peter, suffering alongside many other believers, including Paul. This tidal wave of persecution rose in part because Nero blamed Christians for the fire of Rome in AD 64. The primary occasion for Peter's second letter seems to have been the denial of Jesus's return by detractors who contended that God does not intervene in human history. Peter rebuts this argument from both personal experience and proven biblical history. On a personal level, he witnessed Jesus's glory at Jesus's *first* coming— the transfiguration. With regard to biblical history, God intervened through a universal flood attested in Scripture (not to mention creation). Thus, as the psalmist stated, with God a thousand years are like a single day (3:8; cf. Ps. 90:4); divine and human reckoning of time is vastly different. While Jesus's return may seem to be delayed, it will assuredly occur at God's appointed time.

In the list of virtues in 2 Peter 1:3–11, Peter indicates once again that it is *God's own character* that is the basis for all true virtue wrought in believers' lives. What's more, it is *his* divine power and the knowledge of *him* through a vital, saving relationship with Jesus Christ in the power of the Spirit that enable believers to pursue those virtues. Yet virtuous living does not happen automatically. Virtue takes deliberate effort. Therefore, believers are expected to make every effort to supplement their faith with specific virtues. Peter's list includes traits that are not easily quantifiable but are nonetheless demonstrable in the growing Christian; they will be manifest to those with whom he or she comes into contact. Believers are to pursue the virtues of moral excellence, knowledge, self-control, steadfastness, godliness, brotherly affection, and love. There is intentionality in the pursuit of these qualities, and there is a definite goal—effectiveness in the service of our Lord Jesus Christ.

This pursuit of godly virtues is grounded in God's own glory and excellence:

> On the basis of God's call extended to believers to (or by) his own glory and excellence (2 Pet. 1:3), [believers] should respond by adding to their faith a variety of virtues, starting with excellence (2 Pet. 1:5). This casting of God's character as the starting point and the end goal, setting the agenda for what Christians should pursue, pervades all of Scripture.[2]

It is believers' knowledge of God through the Lord Jesus Christ that is the basis for this endeavor. Indeed, believers' pursuit of Christian virtues is grounded in their relationship with the Lord Jesus Christ, as they identify with Jesus and the cross in all of its entailments. Though effort is the operational term in this command, this passage also indicates that these virtues are to be added to one's faith as grounded "in God's gracious promises." This means that the effort believers supply should not be exerted in their own strength but should be based on God's grace and empowered by the Spirit. Virtuous living is undergirded by trust and even rest in God's provision. Believers' attitude will be that of waiting upon the Lord, listening to his leading, and responding to the ongoing work of the Spirit in their lives, turning to God in a reliant, prayerful attitude.

This call to pursue virtue, of course, presupposes the salvation of the individual believer. The introduction to 1 Peter identifies the readers as "those who have obtained a faith of equal standing with ours by the *righteousness* of our God and Savior Jesus Christ" (2 Pet. 1:1). Righteousness matters to God. Godliness and growth in

---

2. Andreas J. Köstenberger, *Excellence: The Character of God and the Pursuit of Scholarly Virtue* (Wheaton, IL: Crossway, 2011), 45.

Christlikeness are not optional; they are to be a central priority in believers' lives. They are being prepared for eternity in a "new heavens and a new earth in which righteousness dwells" (2 Pet. 3:13). In addition, the readers are told that as a result of the deliberate practice of adding virtues to their faith, their experience in the Lord will be fruitful—they will be kept from being unproductive in their service to the Lord (1:8). Not only will the outcome be fruitfulness in relationships and ministry; this growth of character will be evidence of the salvation they have obtained. Thus, in an intriguing dynamic, believers participate in their own spiritual growth by adding virtues to their faith without which there would be no evidence or assurance of final salvation which was given to them by grace in the first place.

It bears repeating that a believer's *character* is the core for fruitful service to the Lord. It is not so much *what* a believer does, how often they attend church, how much they give, or what they say—though these are all very important. What matters most is that these activities are based on true, robust spiritual character issuing from a growing relationship with Christ. True and effective ministry will flourish in the presence of the quality of a believer's character as he or she relates to those around him or her. The presence of virtuous character will also be the proof or assurance that our relationship with the Lord is real and vibrant, leading to ultimate salvation. Unfortunately, however, virtue is often absent in contemporary discussions of discipleship. While terminology may differ, in virtue-oriented approaches to discipleship there is "a consistent emphasis on the priority of *being* over *doing.* It does little good to emphasize what is right and wrong if people are not developing the inward character that will result in their choice of what is right. . . . In the end, of course, being and doing sustain a close relationship. A person's actions reveal his or her character, while character produces actions. Jesus [himself] affirms that it is out of the abundance of the heart that the mouth speaks (Matt. 12:34; Luke 6:45)."[3] Life in the Spirit, entered by God's gracious initiative and empowered by his sustaining grace, results in our resolved effort.

John's Legacy: The Supremacy of Love

Toward the end of his life, in the early 90s AD, the apostle John wrote three letters to congregations under his care. Tradition suggests these were located in Ephesus in the province of Asia Minor. In his first letter John strikes a note of realism over against opponents who denied the reality of sin and therefore the need for the atonement. He stresses the importance of "walk[ing] in the light" (1 John 1:7), that is, of living moral lives in keeping with believers' call to holiness. As a result, they will enjoy fellowship with other believers and experience continual cleansing by the blood of Jesus. Conversely, if they claim to be sinless (as perfectionists do), they are self-deceived. Not only this, they make God out to be a liar, because his word makes clear that humanity in fact sinned (1:5–10). Of course, believers should make every effort not to sin; but if they do, they "have an advocate with the Father, Jesus Christ the righteous. He is the propitiation for our sins" (2:1–2; cf. 4:10). The bottom line is this: "Whoever says he abides in him ought to walk in the same way in which he walked" (2:6).

In what follows, John elaborates that this includes living by Jesus's "new commandment" of loving fellow believers (1 John 2:7–11). At the same time, believers are not to "love the world or the things in the world" (2:15–17). In this way, John conceives of the entirety of the Christian life as revolving around properly aligning one's affections so that one loves what is good and shuns what is evil. John also affirms believers' identity as God's children, in contrast to the world that does not know him (3:1–2). He quickly adds,

---

3. Köstenberger, *Excellence*, 46–47.

however, that "everyone who thus hopes in him *purifies himself as he is pure*" (3:3). Again, we see here the obligation on the part of believers to engage in an active pursuit of purity and holiness as a result of their conferred status as God's children. Another practical aspect of living out one's Christian calling is engaging in acts of charity; in this way, we will "not [merely] love in word or talk but in deed and in truth" (3:17–18). Again, Jesus set the ultimate example by giving his life for believers; as his followers, they should be prepared to similarly serve others voluntarily and sacrificially.

John expresses one stunning implication of this when he says, "No one has ever seen God; if we love one another, God abides in us and his love is perfected in us" (1 John 4:12). In other words, as believers relate to other Christians in a loving way, the world will be able to see God's love through them. People in the world cannot see God *directly*, but they can see him *indirectly* through believers' *love for others*. This suggests that believers should love others not merely for the sake of enjoying warm and encouraging relationships within the body; rather, love also has an important redemptive and missional dimension. Many have, in fact, become Christians, at least in part, because of the love they saw in believers relating to one another. So, then, love is the cardinal virtue believers ought to pursue. In this, John concurs with Paul who puts love first in listing the fruit of the Spirit (Gal. 5:22)—not to mention the "love chapter," 1 Corinthians 13—and Peter, who climaxes his list of Christian virtues with love (2 Pet. 3:7).

John adds another important truth when he writes, "No one who abides in him keeps on sinning; no one who keeps on sinning has either seen him or known him" (1 John 3:6). While believers are not sinless and therefore need to keep confessing their sins (1:9), they will not "keep on sinning"—that is, continue to live in sin—in large part because they have been born again and received the Holy Spirit, and the Spirit in them will prompt them to live righteously and remove sin from their lives. Conversely, if anyone "keeps on sinning," such a person has neither seen him nor known him. Thus, believers must be discerning: not everyone who claims to be a Christian necessarily is. They should not be unduly gullible and believe every "profession of faith," especially if it is not accompanied by evidence of Christian character.

John ends with the exhortation, "Little children, keep yourselves from idols" (1 John 5:21). This comes on the heels of John's affirmation, "We know that we are from God, and the whole world lies in the power of the evil one" (5:19). In this way, John calls for clear spiritual separation from the world. Believers cannot have one foot in the world and another in God's kingdom. As Jesus said, "No one can serve two masters" (Matt. 6:24). Even in a Christian's life, there may still be idolatry, defined as placing inordinate affection on the things of this world, whether material possessions, improper relationships, or a variety of other attachments (1 John 2:15). What stirs impurity in you? Search your heart for inordinate desires and ask God to set you free from them; at the same time, actively renounce them and set your heart on loving God and his kingdom. As Jesus said, "Seek first the kingdom of God and his righteousness, and all these things will be added to you" (Matt. 6:33). A life of holiness is a life of pure devotion to the one true God.

Final Sanctification

Revelation, like John's Gospel and letters, shows the summing up of human history and thus also the final product of humanity's sanctification in Christ. Believers eagerly await the final, perfect state where there will be no more crying, death, mourning, or pain (Rev. 21:4). There will be no more sin, and we will be clothed with glorified, perfect bodies and live eternally in God's presence. All of God's covenant promises will have come to fruition, as the repetition of the Bible's "covenant formula" indicates: "They will be his people, and God himself will be with them and be their God" (21:3). So, on a canonical level, the book of Revelation depicts the consummation of the age and the fulfillment of God's plan for humanity and the world in Christ. In the meantime, John writes, "Let the evildoer still do evil, and the filthy still be filthy, and the righteous still do right, and the *holy* still *be holy*" (22:11).

As in the early portions of Scripture, such as in the Levitical holiness code, Revelation depicts God as eternally and utterly holy (Rev. 4:8: "Holy, holy, holy"; 6:10: "O Sovereign Lord, holy and true"). Thus God's holiness is shown to span the ages and all of human history. The one thing that never changes is the eternal holiness of God. While created in a garden, humanity's ultimate destiny is the celestial city, the new Jerusalem, "the holy city" (Rev. 11:2; 21:2, 10; 22:19). The beauty of holiness is on full display when the seer depicts Jerusalem as "the holy city, new Jerusalem, coming down out of heaven from God, prepared as a bride, adorned for her husband" (Rev. 21:2). In contrast to the Old Testament portrayal of the exclusivity of the priesthood, Revelation presents all believers as a royal priesthood with God's name on their forehead (Rev. 22:4). While the high priest entered the Most Holy Place only once a year, with God's name on his forehead (Ex. 28:38), believers will be able to approach God's throne and see his face unhindered for all eternity.

While we wait for God's glorious consummation of all things, we still have the responsibility to make holiness a priority. This also means we should be devoted to prayer, since the "prayers of the saints" are shown to be effective, including prayers for God's vindication of their suffering at the hands of a godless, evil world ruled by Satan (Rev. 5:8; 8:3–4). At the center of the vision, the *positional* and *progressive* dimensions of sanctification are on full display: believers are those who "have conquered [Satan, the accuser of the brethren] by the blood of the Lamb and by the word of their testimony, for they loved not their lives even unto death" (12:11). Because of Christ's atoning and interceding work, none of Satan's accusations can stand against those whom God has made holy. Because of his empowering presence in the Spirit, his holy people witness to Christ and follow his call to forsake their own lives.

Summary

We concluded our study of the New Testament teaching on sanctification with later New Testament writings that address the cultivation of various Christian virtues. We saw how Paul urges his apostolic delegates to set the example of godliness for all believers, exhorting them to pursue various godly virtues "together with all those who call on God with a pure heart" (2 Tim. 2:22). This reminds us that growing in Christ is not a solitary pursuit but is done in community with proper accountability. We also found specific instructions given to both men and women. Men are commanded to pray in unity and without arguing, while women are held to a standard of purity, self-control, and modesty. We also saw how the idea of God's household underlies Paul's instructions, indicating that more mature believers have a responsibility to mentor to maturity those who are younger. An example of this instruction is Titus 2, which calls on mature and reverent women to mentor younger women in godly living, including loving their husbands and children.

Jude addresses his letter to those "called, beloved in God and kept for Jesus Christ" (Jude 1). He reminds them of their obligation to defend "the faith that was once for all delivered to the saints" (3) and to show mercy on those who doubt or struggle. In a stirring doxology, Jude affirms that God is able to keep believers from stumbling and to present them *blameless* in God's presence. In 2 Peter, Peter urges believers to add to their faith a series of Christian virtues. This puts the spotlight on the vital importance of Christian character (being) rather than merely engaging in various Christian activities (doing).

Our study of John's first letter yielded several interesting insights regarding sanctification. Specifically, we saw John highlight the importance of "walk[ing] in the light" (1 John 1:7) while being realistic about the fact that believers still occasionally sin. John also stresses the importance of love, not only in order to encourage caring relationships among believers but also because love among believers will be a powerful testimony to unbelievers of God's love for them in Christ. Finally, John urged believers to flee idolatry, that is, to avoid setting improper affections on the things of this world. Again, the vertical call to holiness manifests itself in horizontal relationships, both positively and negatively: those set apart by God in Christ are called to care for one another and renounce the temptations of the world.

Revelation, finally, presents the ultimate outcome of sanctification. In heaven, there will no longer be any suffering, pain, or death, just as all sin will be forever banished from God's presence. All believers will receive glorified bodies so they can spend eternity in God's presence. Believers should continue to live holy lives, knowing that one day God will remove all evil from his—and their—presence. Imagine a day when there will be no more temptation, no more struggle against sin, no more Satan to combat! Hard to imagine, we know, but Scripture says it's true. The bedrock of our hope in this promise is the finished work of Christ who has conquered the accuser with his atoning blood. Thus believers witness to Christ in word and deed, "[loving] not their lives even unto death" (12:11). Positional sanctification sets believers on a continual path of progressive sanctification.

7

Practice

New Life in Christ

We've engaged in a historical, literary, and theological survey of sanctification in both Testaments. Now let's briefly synthesize our findings and move toward application. While many of these topics surfaced repeatedly throughout our study, it will be helpful to gather them here and discuss them topically. Relevant topics include union with Christ and abiding in Christ; suffering and discipline; the sovereignty of the Holy Spirit in sanctification; community and mission; and, last but not least, marriage, family, and mentoring. Not only are these sanctification-related topics prominent throughout Scripture; they are also essential to consider when working out the practical aspects of sanctification.

A New Way of Life

In the Old Testament, Israel's experience of God depended on intermittent sacrifices made by priests who were themselves sinful and destined to die and be replaced. Apart from the temporary nature of the priests and their offerings, the sacrificial system was insufficient because of the power of sin in people's hearts. As a result, the people of Israel regularly failed to live holy lives in response to their holy God. At the same time, the Old Testament testifies to God's passionate commitment to his people. In the New Testament, a new way of life in the Spirit emerges that was impossible prior to Christ's coming. While God was ever-present, powerful, and faithful to his people throughout history, it is only in Christ that believers can avail themselves of God's provision of abiding forgiveness and new spiritual life. Nevertheless, the Old Testament is preparatory for what takes place in the New:

> Just as Paul saw the Torah as designed to point the way towards Christ (Gal. 3:24), so too Jerusalem's role was inherently preparatory. When the one came who would offer himself outside its walls as a sacrifice for sin, its sacrificial system would not be required. When the one came who would embody the incarnate presence of God, the true *shekinah* presence, then the Temple as the previously focused location of the divine name would need to be laid aside. When the Spirit came, Jerusalem's role as witnessing to the presence of God in the midst of his people would no longer be necessary.[1]

What is more, not only was there redemption in Christ and power for holy living in the Spirit, but this new way of life also entailed a vital missional dimension:

> When the time came when the gospel could go out "to all nations," then the previous particularity associated with

---

1. Peter W. L. Walker, *Jesus and the Holy City: New Testament Perspectives on Jerusalem* (Grand Rapids, MI: Eerdmans, 1996), 315.

Jerusalem would need to give way. When Gentiles could at last enter the "people of God," then the necessary distinction between Jew and Gentile emblazoned within the temple, would have to be "broken down." Finally, when the full revelation of God in Christ was made known and the glories of his heavenly Jerusalem could be glimpsed, then the previous symbolic role of Jerusalem as encapsulating God's final purpose for his world could be seen to have truly fulfilled its purpose.[2]

Union with Christ

Union with Christ is the substance of Paul's "in Christ" language and Jesus's call to "abide" in John's Gospel. Believers' participation with Christ in his death and resurrection is thus the basis for the Spirit's work of positional sanctification at conversion and progressive sanctification throughout believers' lives. As the Puritan John Owen explains, "Sanctification is an *immediate* work of the Spirit of God on the souls of believer[s], purifying their natures from the pollution and uncleanness of sin, *renewing* in them the image of God, and thereby enabling them, from a spiritual and habitual principle of grace, to *yield obedience* to God, according to the tenor of the new covenant, by virtue of the life and death of Jesus Christ."[3] Union with Christ thus encompasses the cluster of related spiritual realities that occur at the time of conversion. While the order of events that occur at conversion is of some interest, union with Christ, in general terms, is *the overall reality of identifying with Christ in his death, burial, and resurrection by faith.* This reality, in turn, allows believers to participate in the spiritual blessings and work of the Spirit.

---

2. Walker, *Jesus and the Holy City*, 315.

3. John Owen, *Holy Spirit: His Gifts and Power* (Fearn, Ross-shire, UK: Christian Focus, 2004), 257.

The Sovereignty of the Spirit in Sanctification

Sanctification is a sovereign work of the Holy Spirit. Nevertheless, it involves committed and dedicated participation. In definitive, positional sanctification, the Spirit sets the believer apart from sin and the world and for God and his service. Then, in progressive sanctification, the Spirit is continually at work in believers, both individually and corporately, to cleanse them from sin and make them more like Christ. Paul stresses the pivotal nature of the Spirit's work in sanctification. As he states in Romans, believers live under a new "law," the "law of the Spirit." To the Galatians, he writes that just as they began by the Spirit when they received the Spirit, they are continually to "walk in the Spirit," be "led by the Spirit," "keep in step with the Spirit," and increasingly display the "fruit of the Spirit" (Gal. 5). While believers have a responsibility to yield to and collaborate with the Spirit, sanctification is ultimately the work of the Spirit, not that of believers. Thus sanctification is not a synergistic work in which the Spirit and the believer collaborate on equal terms. Rather, it is the indwelling Spirit who does his work in believers as they continually respond to his divine initiative, causing them both "to will and to work for his good pleasure" (Phil. 2:13). Sanctification is a sovereign work of God's Spirit.

Discipline and Suffering

Sanctification is also integrally related to discipline and suffering. The Christian life is about dying to self, which is a form of suffering. As Jesus told his disciples, "If anyone would come after me, let him deny himself and take up his cross and follow me" (Mark 8:34). At the same time, Jesus invited people with these hopeful words: "Come to me, all who labor and are heavy laden, and I will give you rest. Take my yoke upon you, and learn from me, for I am gentle and lowly in heart, and you will find rest for your souls. For my yoke is easy, and my burden is light" (Matt. 11:28–30). God uses suffering as a form of discipline for our good (Heb. 12:5–17). We should welcome such divine discipline, knowing that it will produce Christlike character in us. The exhortation extends to us today: "Let us run with endurance the race that is set before us, looking to Jesus, the founder and perfecter of our faith, who for the joy that was set before him endured the cross, despising the shame, and is seated at the right hand of the throne of God" (Heb. 12:1–3).

Peter echoes these thoughts, emphasizing that Christ set the supreme example of how to suffer when dying for us on the cross. Thus we should walk in his footsteps, entrusting ourselves to our faithful Creator, who judges righteously and will vindicate us in the end (1 Pet. 2:21–25). Peter makes clear that righteous suffering has great rewards and is supremely Christlike (3:8–18). The theme of suffering also surfaces repeatedly in Revelation. The persecuted believers cry out for God to end their suffering and to vindicate them against the unbelieving world that had subjected some of them to martyrdom. While they were victims of injustice, their ultimate victory is sure. Contrary to how it might appear, God sees our suffering and will hold those who harmed us fully accountable on judgment day. In the meantime, if called to do so, we can glorify God in our righteous suffering.

We live in a fallen, sinful world, and sanctification inevitably takes place in a context which is anything but perfect. Yet God can use even injustice to accomplish his righteous ends, as we see supremely demonstrated at the cross. There is no virtue in suffering for suffering's sake, and we sometimes suffer the consequences of our own poor actions. However, believers will often suffer for the cause of Christ or even for no apparent earthly reason. Like Jesus, we should put our trust in God even when we don't know why we're suffering. We may not know the answer on this side of eternity, but God will always be worthy of our trust, because he is a good God who allows suffering to refine and purify our faith in him. We must also remember that Christ suffered on our behalf and, as Isaiah wrote, is intimately acquainted with grief (Isa. 53:3–4). We can entrust ourselves to him and be comforted by the fact that he knows and will be with us in our struggles.

Community and Mission

Especially in an individualistic culture, there is a great temptation to view sanctification primarily as an individual pursuit: Bible reading, prayer, fasting, journaling, and other spiritual disciplines are often assumed to be solo endeavors. While each individual Christian has a responsibility to grow in Christ, sanctification is not primarily presented in Scripture as a self-orchestrated, individual pursuit. Rather, the primary arena for sanctification is the community of faith, the church, under the leadership of mature, qualified pastors and elders. In Ephesians, Paul calls on the *community* of believers to be filled with the Spirit. While this community consists of individual, Spirit-filled believers, it is significant that Paul's primary reference is to a Spirit-indwelt community that sings God's praises and engages in God-honoring relationships.

What's more, sanctification is not an end in itself, whether individually or corporately. We don't merely engage in sanctification so we become more mature or our church grows more spiritual. This would only foster spiritual pride. Not only is salvation by grace, but so is sanctification; and in this miraculous work of God, no one can boast. Rather, sanctification takes place ultimately to spread God's glory, which is our primary mission. We've seen this mission unfold especially in John's Gospel, and there foremost in Jesus's final prayer. The Father consecrated Jesus and set him apart for his mission in this world; similarly, once Jesus accomplished his redemptive mission, he consecrated and commissioned his new messianic community and sent his followers into the world to proclaim the gospel with these words: "As the Father sent me, even so I am sending you" (John 20:21). To be sure, mutual love and unity are indispensable prerequisites for mission; but these were never meant to be ends in themselves. Sanctification comes at God's initiative, continues by God's power, and culminates in God's glory.

Marriage, Family, and Mentoring

We've already touched on the important communal dimension of sanctification. Under the previous heading, we focused primarily on the church and her mission to the world. Here, we focus our attention on a vital sphere of sanctification: marriage and family. In Ephesians, Paul calls on believers to be filled with the Spirit (5:18). Only three verses later, we see how this filling impacts the marriage relationship: wives are to submit to their husbands as the church submits to Christ, and husbands are to love their wives as Christ loved the church (5:21–29).[4] This command presupposes that both wife and husband are Spirit-filled.

In our treatment of Paul's letters to Timothy and Titus, we've seen how Paul depicts the church as God's household. As believers, we've not only been adopted individually by God; we've been inducted into the spiritual family of God. This further implies that, as in the natural household, there will be spiritual "fathers" and "mothers" as well as "brothers" and "sisters." In other words, mentoring will invariably take place, and should intentionally take place, as mature and experienced believers help younger believers grow in their faith.

---

4. Andreas J. Köstenberger and Margaret E. Köstenberger, *God's Design for Man and Woman: A Biblical-Theological Survey* (Wheaton, IL: Crossway, 2014), 180–90.

Notice also that in Ephesians 6, family relationships are set in the context of spiritual warfare. Thus, as part of our growth and experience in the Lord, we must put on the full armor of God. Significantly, the command to put on God's armor is not addressed to people generically but in the context of the various kinds of relationships in which they are engaged: wives and husbands, fathers and mothers, children and parents. As Paul reminds us, our struggle is not against flesh and blood but against the devil and his minions who are out to destroy God's good creation and subvert his design for man and woman.

Conclusion

David asked, "Who shall ascend the hill of the LORD? And who shall stand in his holy place?" (Ps. 24:3). The God of eternal holiness, set apart in the excellence of his being, demands heartfelt obedience and moral excellence from his called-out people. God's fallen image bearers have failed to uphold his holy standards and reflect his perfection. In Christ, however, they've been given access to perfect holiness and the power of God's grace. In Christ, they partake of his holy blessings and receive redemption and forgiveness of sins. In Christ, believers are *positionally* sanctified through the gift of the indwelling Holy Spirit and empowered to work out their salvation in *progressive* sanctification, propelled toward moral excellence, missional community, and meaningful relationships. In Christ, they are assured of future *perfect* sanctification when glorified in his presence. In Christ, they desist from dead works and start living a new life—life in the Spirit.

As sanctified and Spirit-filled believers, we've become part of God's mission to bring his name and saving message to the ends of the earth as we witness boldly to the one who lives inside us. Holiness is inherent to God's nature and therefore central to our witness as we boldly identify with him. While set apart for him and granted great power through him in the Spirit, we're still on a journey of growth and renewal until he comes again and completes our sanctification. As John wrote, "See what kind of love the Father has given to us, that we should be called children of God; and so we are. . . . Beloved, we are God's children now, and what we will be has not yet appeared; but we know that when he appears we shall be like him, because we shall see him as he is. And everyone who thus hopes in him purifies himself as he is pure" (1 John 3:1–3).

For Further Reading

Alexander, Don, ed. *Christian Spirituality: Five Views of Sanctification.* Downers Grove, IL: IVP Academic, 1989.

Allen, Michael. *Sanctification.* New Studies in Dogmatics. Grand Rapids, MI: Zondervan, 2017.

Allison, Gregg R. *Embodied: Living as Whole People in a Fractured World.* Grand Rapids, MI: Baker, 2021.

Allison, Gregg R., and Andreas J. Köstenberger. *The Holy Spirit.* Theology for the People of God. Nashville, TN: B&H Academic, 2020.

Campbell, Constantine R. *Paul and Union with Christ: An Exegetical and Theological Study.* Grand Rapids, MI: Zondervan, 2012.

DeYoung, Kevin. *The Hole in Our Holiness.* Wheaton, IL: Crossway, 2012.

Dieter, Melvin E., Anthony A. Hoekema, Stanley M. Horton, J. Robertson McQuilkin, and John F. Walvoord. *Five Views on Sanctification.* Counterpoints: Bible and Theology. Grand Rapids, MI: Zondervan, 1996.

Dunson, Ben C. "Biblical Words and Theological Meanings: Sanctification as Consecration for Transformation." *Themelios* 44, no. 1 (2019): 70–88.

Gentry, Peter J. "The Meaning of 'Holy' in the Old Testament." *Bibliotheca sacra* 170, no. 680 (2013): 400–17.

Gentry, Peter J. "Sizemore Lectures: No One Holy Like the Lord." *Midwestern Journal of Theology* 12, no. 1 (2013): 17–38.

Hawthorne, Gerald F. "Holy, Holiness." In *Dictionary of the Later New Testament and Its Developments*, edited by Ralph P. Martin and Peter H. Davids, 485–89. Downers Grove, IL: IVP Academic, 1997.

Köstenberger, Andreas J. "Abide." In *Dictionary of Jesus and the Gospels*, 2nd ed., edited by Joel B. Green, Jeannine K. Brown, and Nicholas Perrin, 1–2. Downers Grove, IL: IVP Academic, 2013.

Köstenberger, Andreas J. *Excellence: The Character of God and the Pursuit of Scholarly Virtue*. Wheaton, IL: Crossway, 2011.

Köstenberger, Andreas J. "What Does It Mean to Be Filled with the Holy Spirit?" *Journal of the Evangelical Theological Society* 40 (1997): 229–40.

Owen, John. *Holy Spirit: His Gifts and Power*. Fearn, Ross-shire, UK: Christian Focus, 2004.

Peterson, David G. "Holiness." In *New Dictionary of Biblical Theology*, edited by T. Desmond Alexander and Brian S. Rosner, 544–50. Downers Grove, IL: IVP Academic, 2000.

Peterson, David G. *Possessed by God: A New Testament Theology of Sanctification and Holiness*. New Studies in Biblical Theology. Downers Grove, IL: InterVarsity Press, 1995.

Porter, Steve L. "Holiness, Sanctification." In *Dictionary of Paul and His Letters*, edited by Gerald F. Hawthorne, Ralph P. Martin, and Daniel G. Reid, 397–402. Downers Grove, IL: IVP Academic, 1993.

Porter, Steve L. "Sanctification." In *Dictionary of Christian Spirituality*, edited by Glen G. Scorgie, 734. Grand Rapids, MI: Zondervan, 2011.

Tabb, Brian J. *All Things New: Revelation as Canonical Capstone*. New Studies in Biblical Theology. Downers Grove, IL: InterVarsity Press, 2019.

General Index

abiding in Christ, 40–44, 119
Abraham, 57; justified by faith, 78
Abrahamic covenant, 15, 23
Acts, 50–52, 64
antinomianism, 78
armor of God, 124

Bavinck, Herman, 10n16
Beatitudes, 34
believers, as royal priesthood, 114
biblical theology, of sanctification, 4–5
blameless, 107
blasphemy, 39

Calvin, John, 3
character, 54, 110
Christian freedom, 60
Christian identity, 70–71
Christian life, 60, 65
Christian virtues, 115
Christlikeness, 93, 110
church: development and maturation of, 49; as Spirit-filled temple of God, 84–85, 87
cleansing, 40
community: and mission, 122–23; as Spirit-filled, 83–85; unity of, 46
complete sanctification, 63

consecration, 10, 17, 29; of the temple, 21
consecration and commission of followers of Christ, 33–36, 39, 45–46, 47
covenant formula, 114
Cretans, 105–6
Cyrus, 22

Davidic covenant, 19–20, 23
dead to sin and alive to God, 79
devotion to God, 16–17, 18–19
DeYoung, Kevin, 3
disciples, bearing fruit, 43
discipleship, 47
discipline, 95, 120–22
"dwelling of God," 83–85

early church, 50–53, 64
Edwards, Jonathan, 12–13
elect exiles, 99
endurance, 54
Enoch, 61
entire sanctification, 3
Ephesians, 83
eternal security, 83
exile, 20, 22
Ezekiel, 21–22, 23–24
Ezra, 22

Scripture Index

Short Studies in Biblical Theology Series

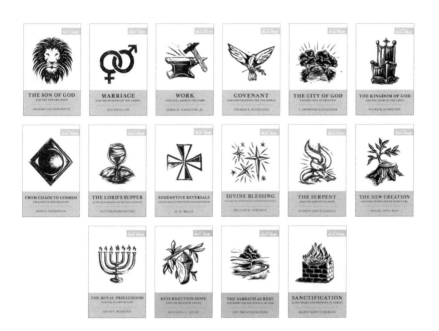

For more information, visit **crossway.org/ssbt**.